# SQL

MIKE McGRATH

**In easy steps** is an imprint of Computer Step
Southfield Road . Southam
Warwickshire CV47 0FB . United Kingdom
www.ineasysteps.com

**Notice of Liability**

Every effort has been made to ensure that this book contains accurate and current information. However, Computer Step and the author shall not be liable for any loss or damage suffered by readers as a result of any information contained herein.

**Trademarks**

All trademarks are acknowledged as belonging to their respective companies.

Printed and bound in the United Kingdom

ISBN 1-84078-296-X

# Contents

# Retrieving data from tables

**5**

# Sorting retrieved data

**6**

# Simple data filtering

**7**

# Complex data filtering

**8**

# Generating calculated fields

**9**

# Conventions in this book

SQL keywords (those words that have special meaning in the Structured Query Language) appear in uppercase like this:

SELECT

Examples of SQL query syntax appear within this type of box:

```
CREATE TABLE  table-name  ;
```

The italicized text in the query is a place-holder indicating where an SQL object name should appear. In this case the place-holder would be replaced by the actual name of a table in a real query.

SQL sample code appears in a different font to regular text and looks like this:

```
# Use the default MySQL database
USE mysql;

# List the MySQL database tables
SHOW TABLES;
```

The actual SQL code to be processed is shown in bold whereas the explanatory comments are normal weight.

Each code sample is identified by a file name below the icon that appears alongside the code, like this:

*select-col.sql*

For the convenience of readers, all the SQL sample files listed in this book can be downloaded from this book's page on the publisher's website at http://www.ineasysteps.com

# Introducing SQL

Welcome to the exciting topic of Structured Query Language (SQL) - the world's most widely used database language.

This chapter describes the evolution of SQL and shows how SQL queries can be made from a variety of popular software. It demonstrates how to acquire and install a free database server – both on Windows and Linux operating systems. There is also an introduction to Open DataBase Connectivity (ODBC) and the Microsoft Query tool for SQL.

## Covers

Chapter One

# What is SQL ?

The Structured Query Language (SQL) is a language designed specifically for communicating with databases. Today, SQL (pronounced either "S-Q-L" or "sequel") is the industry-wide standard language used by virtually all database systems.

Databases allow collections of data to be stored in an organized manner – in the same way that data can be stored in an organized way inside files within a filing cabinet. Most modern Database Management Systems (DBMS') store data in related tables, so are called relational DBMS'. The data stored inside databases can be examined and manipulated by SQL commands.

SQL commands are known as "queries" and utilize special keywords that can be used both to add data to a database, or extract details of data contained within a database. There are not many keywords so SQL is simple to understand but, despite its apparent simplicity, is a powerful language. Clever use of its language components enable complex sophisticated database operations to be performed.

## The evolution of SQL

The model for the basis of SQL was defined back in 1970 by Dr. E. F. Todd, a researcher for IBM, in a paper entitled "A Relational Model of Data for Large Shared Data Banks". This article generated a great deal of interest in the feasibility of producing a practical commercial application of such a system.

IBM really began to develop these ideas in 1974 when they started the System/R project which eventually created the Structured English Query Language (SEQUEL). This was rewritten in 1976 to include multi-table and multi-user features and was renamed SQL in 1978. During this time other software companies had begun working on database systems based upon the SQL model. Most notable of these were Oracle, Sybase and Ingres (from the University of California's Berkeley Ingres project). The first to be released commercially was Oracle in 1979. IBM released improved database products named SQL/DS in 1982 and DB2 in 1983.

Modern versions of Oracle, Sybase, Ingres and DB2 DBMS' are available today and are in widespread use around the world.

## Standardization of SQL

In order to clarify the precise nature of SQL, so that it could be implemented universally, each aspect of the language was defined by the American National Standards Institute (ANSI). They first published a standard specification in 1989, known as SQL-89. The SQL-89 specification was expanded three years later with the publication of the SQL-92 specification by a joint committee of ANSI and the International Standards Organization (ISO). A third ANSI/ISO standard specification, SQL-99, was introduced in 1999 to address issues of advanced SQL syntax – but all the core features remained the same as in the SQL-92 specification. Some DBMS vendors have added proprietary features to the ANSI-defined SQL standard. These extended versions even have their own names, such as PL-SQL and Transact-SQL. The examples given in this book mostly use standard ANSI-SQL so they can be applied to any DBMS irrespective of brand.

*"ISO" is not an acronym but is derived from the Greek word "isos" meaning equal – as in "isometric".*

## Forms of SQL query

There are a number of ways that SQL queries may be sent to a database to deposit or extract data:

*Learning standard ANSI-SQL enables you to interact with every major database there is.*

- Directly input through an integral SQL-client application that is part of the DBMS package – this is the most straightforward method and is used in this book to demonstrate SQL features

- Input through a third-party SQL-client application – this method communicates with the database via an intermediate software "driver". On Windows systems these are typically Open DataBase Connectivity (ODBC) data source drivers

- From a script – often found on web servers to dynamically communicate with a database using a scripting language such as PERL or PHP

- From an Integrated Development Environment (IDE) – programmers using IDEs, such as Microsoft Visual Basic, can build programs that incorporate SQL queries to a database

The next two pages outline how to execute SQL queries using a variety of popular software.

# Making SQL queries

### Oracle®

The Oracle DBMS is popular and widely used in commerce.
In Oracle 8 and Oracle 9 there is a management tool called
Enterprise Manager that contains a feature named SQL Worksheet.
This is where SQL queries can be entered for execution against a
database:

1.  Launch Enterprise Manager then select SQL Worksheet.
2.  When prompted for login details, enter a valid user name
    and password to connect to the database server.
3.  The SQL Worksheet comprises two panes. Type an SQL
    query into the lower pane then click the Execute button.
4.  The results of the query are then shown in the upper pane

### IBM® DB2®

The DB2 DBMS is a powerful multi-platform system that is
supplied with a comprehensive suite of tools. This includes the
Query Management Facility (QMF) that allows SQL queries to be
entered for execution against a database:

*ISPF stands for
Interactive
System
Productivity
Facility.*

1.  First select QMF from the ISPF menu.
2.  Next press F6 to access the QMF Query Panel.
3.  Type an SQL query into the QMF Query Panel.
4.  Press F2 to execute the query.
5.  The results of the query are then displayed on the screen.

### Microsoft® SQL Server 7/SQL Server 2000

These SQL Server DBMS products from Microsoft are popular on
computers running the Windows operating system. They offer an
impressive range of features – including a tool called SQL Query
Analyzer that can be used to make SQL queries in a database:

1.  Launch SQL Query Analyzer from the SQL Server group.
2.  When prompted for login details, enter a valid username
    and password to connect to the database server.
3.  The Query screen will open. Select the database from the
    drop-down DB menu on the toolbar.
4.  Type an SQL query into the large text window.
5.  Press F5 to execute the query.
6.  The results of the query are displayed in a separate pane.

### Microsoft® Access

Access is, of course, the popular database program supplied as part of the Microsoft Office suite. It is popular with Office users on stand-alone PCs and small networks. It includes a Query Designer tool that allows SQL queries to be made against an open database:

1.  Launch Access and open a database to work with.
2.  Select Queries in the Database window's Objects list.
3.  Click on the New button and select Design View.
4.  Simply close the Show Table dialog box that appears.
5.  Select SQL View on the main View menu.
6.  Type an SQL query into the revealed Query window.
7.  Select Run on the main Query menu to execute the query.
8.  The Query window changes from SQL View to Datasheet View and displays the results of the query.

### Microsoft® Visual Basic

Visual Basic 6 also includes a Visual Data manager that can be used to enter SQL queries against a database via an ODBC Data Source:

1.  Launch Visual Basic then select Visual Data Manager from the main Add-Ins menu. This opens a VisData window.
2.  Select Open DataBase in the VisData window's File menu then choose the ODBC item in the sub-menu.
3.  Click the arrowed button in the ODBC Logon window to reveal the list of available ODBC Data Sources.
4.  Select the appropriate Data Source for the database to work with then click the OK button.
5.  Type an SQL query into the SQL Statement window.
6.  Click the Execute button to execute the query.
7.  The results of the query appear in a new window.

### MySQL®

The world's most popular open-source database server is the freely available MySQL DBMS product that is supplied with an integral SQL-client. This is used throughout this book to demonstrate the SQL language. The following pages describe how to download and install MySQL on both Windows and Linux platforms.

# Installing MySQL on Windows

There are a variety of database servers available for purchase, such as Microsoft Access, but the MySQL database server is both powerful and free. It is in widespread use on web servers and can be freely downloaded from www.mysql.com.

Download the latest recommended binary release of MySQL for Windows from the web site. This example installation uses the Microsoft Installer version mysql-essential-4.1.10-win32.msi – the installation procedure may vary for other versions.

Run the downloaded file to launch the MySQL Server Setup Wizard. When asked, select the "Typical" installation type and accept the suggested installation location – the MySQL Server files then get installed on your computer.

In the final dialog box of the Setup Wizard check the box to "Configure MySQL Server now" then click the "Finish" button. This closes the Setup Wizard then launches the MySQL Server Configuration Wizard.

Select the "Standard Configuration" option then check all the Windows options in the next dialog box, as shown below:

*In Windows XP the service can be stopped and started using the Management Console – follow* Start | Control Panel | Administrative Tools | Services *to find it.*

---

**MySQL Server Instance Configuration Wizard**

**MySQL Server Instance Configuration**

Configure the MySQL Server 4.1 server instance.

Please set the Windows options.

☑ **Install As Windows Service**

This is the recommended way to run the MySQL server on Windows.

Service Name:　MySQL

☑ Launch the MySQL Server automatically

☑ **Include Bin Directory in Windows PATH**

Check this option to include the directory containing the server / client executables in the Windows PATH variable so they can be called from the command line.

< Back　　Next >　　Cancel

---

Click on the "Next" button to proceed to security options and check the box to "Modify Security Settings" for the root user – the root user has full access privileges to all MySQL databases. Enter a memorable root password which you will use to access the MySQL monitor with full privileges:

**MySQL Server Instance Configuration Wizard**

**MySQL Server Instance Configuration**

Configure the MySQL Server 4.1 server instance.

Please set the security options.

☑ **Modify Security Settings**

New root password: ✱✱✱✱✱✱    Enter the root password.

root    Confirm: ✱✱✱✱✱✱    Retype the password.

☐ Enable root access from remote machines

☐ Create An Anonymous Account

This option will create an anonymous account on this server. Please note that this can lead to an insecure system.

[< Back]  [Next >]  [Cancel]

Click the "Next" button and continue on to complete the configuration. Now launch the MySQL Command Line Client from the MySQL group that has been added to the Windows Start menu and enter your password to open the MySQL monitor:

*Type "exit", "quit" or "\q", then hit Enter to close the MySQL monitor.*

**MySQL Command Line Client**

```
Enter password: ******
Welcome to the MySQL monitor.
Commands end with ; or \g .
Your MySQL connection id is 1 to server version:
4.1.10-nt
Type '\h' for help. Type '\c' to clear the buffer.

mysql>
```

# Installing MySQL on Linux

MySQL for Linux platforms can be freely downloaded from www.mysql.com. The recommended method of installation is to use the Redhat Package Manager (RPM) that is included with virtually all versions of Linux. There are several MySQL RPM packages available for download, similar to this list:

- MySQL 4.1.10 Server (14.6Mb)
- MySQL 4.1.10 Client programs (5.3Mb)
- MySQL 4.1.10 Benchmark/test suites (3.1Mb)
- MySQL 4.1.10 Libraries & header files (2.7Mb)
- MySQL 4.1.10 Dynamic client libraries (1.1Mb)
- MySQL 4.1.10 Embedded server (2.7Mb)

*For installation without using the RPM refer to the MySQL website for instructions.*

The first two packages on this list are required for the basic installation of MySQL – the Server package will run MySQL as a background service and the Client programs package contains the classes to create, and manipulate, databases, tables and records.

This installation example uses MySQL version 4.1.10 – the procedure for other versions may differ.

First download the MySQL-server-4.1.10-0.i386.rpm and the MySQL-client-4.1.10-0.i386.rpm packages together with the MySQL mysql_pubkey.asc signature file. Before installation it's a good idea to verify the files have not been tampered with. As the Linux root user, import the MySQL signature onto the RPM keyring then use the --checksig option to verify the checksums.

```
Linux - Shell - Konsole
Session  Edit  View  Bookmarks  Settings  Help
user> su
Password:
root> ls
MySQL-client-4.1.10-0.i386.rpm
MySQL-server-4.1.10-0.i386.rpm
mysql_pubkey.asc
root> rpm --import mysql_pubkey.asc
root> rpm --checksig MySQL*
MySQL-client-4.1.10-0.i386.rpm: md5 gpg OK
MySQL-server-4.1.10-0.i386.rpm: md5 gpg OK
root> █
```

If both checksums are found to be OK proceed to install the MySQL packages in the usual way:

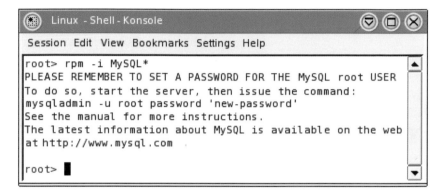

```
root> rpm -i MySQL*
PLEASE REMEMBER TO SET A PASSWORD FOR THE MySQL root USER
To do so, start the server, then issue the command:
mysqladmin -u root password 'new-password'
See the manual for more instructions.
The latest information about MySQL is available on the web
at http://www.mysql.com

root>
```

Notice that the installation displays a reminder to set a password for the MySQL root user. Reboot your computer to start the MySQL server daemon – it will now start automatically whenever the system boots up. Verify it is running using the ping command of the mysqladmin program.

The mysqladmin program can also be used to set the MySQL root user password. In the screenshot below the mysqladmin program specifies that the user (-u) root has the password "rocket". This password (-p) is then used to launch the MySQL monitor with full root user access privileges to all databases.

*Type "exit", "quit" or "\q", then hit Enter to close the MySQL monitor.*

```
user> mysqladmin ping
mysqld is alive
user> mysqladmin -u root password "rocket"
user> mysql -u root -p
Enter password:
Welcome to the MySQL monitor.  Commands end with ; or \g.
Your MySQL connection id is 1 to server version:
4.1.10-standard
Type '\h' for help. Type '\c' to clear the buffer.

mysql> exit
Bye
user>
```

# Installing an ODBC driver

Usually, third-party client applications can only connect to the MySQL server if an appropriate Open DataBase Connectivity (ODBC) driver is installed on the system.

There are a whole range of ODBC drivers for the MySQL server freely available at www.mysql.com for a variety of platforms. This installation example uses a Windows version named MyODBC-3.51.11.1.msi – the procedure may differ for other versions.

*The Microsoft Installer program is included with Windows XP, but can be downloaded from the Microsoft website for other versions.*

Download the ODBC driver installer MyODBC-3.51.11.1.msi and double-click it to begin the installation. Read the information screens as they appear then click "Next" to continue until complete. Nothing appears on the desktop but the driver has now been added to the list of other ODBC drivers on the system. To see these open the ODBC Data Source Administrator – this can be found under Control Panel >Administrative Tools on Windows XP systems and in Control Panel on Windows 9.x systems.

To make the MySQL ODBC driver available system-wide first click on the System DSN tab in the ODBC Data Source Administrator. Now click on the "Add" button to open the Create New Data Source dialog box. Select the MySQL driver from the list of all ODBC drivers then click the "Finish" button.

| Create New Data Source | |
|---|---|

Select a driver for which you want to set up a data source.

| Name | Version |
|---|---|
| Microsoft ODBC for Oracle | 2.573.7713.00 |
| Microsoft Paradox Driver (*.db ) | 4.00.6019.00 |
| Microsoft Paradox-Treiber (*.db ) | 4.00.6019.00 |
| Microsoft Text Driver (*.txt; *.csv) | 4.00.6019.00 |
| Microsoft Text-Treiber (*.txt; *.csv) | 4.00.6019.00 |
| Microsoft Visual FoxPro Driver | 1.00.02.00 |
| Microsoft Visual FoxPro-Treiber | 1.00.02.00 |
| MySQL ODBC 3.51 Driver | 3.51.11.00 |

< Back    Finish    Cancel

The MySQL driver dialog box will appear requesting you to enter a Data Source Name. Type "MySQL Databases" into the text field.

*The default name for a local server is "localhost" and port 3306 is the default port used by the MySQL database server. The database named "test" (and another named "mysql") already exist when MySQL is first installed.*

Complete the other fields then click the "Test" button to test the driver installation. When the installation is successful click the "OK" button to close the MySQL driver dialog box and see the driver appear in the ODBC Data Source Administrator with its given name. The driver is now available system-wide so click the "OK" button to close the ODBC Data Source Administrator.

# Microsoft Query tool

The Microsoft Query tool can be used to make SQL queries to a database. It is installed on many Windows systems without the user even knowing it because it is included with other Microsoft products such as Office. To discover if it is installed, search for a file called msqry32.exe or msquery.exe.

Microsoft Query is a third-party SQL client that requires an ODBC driver to connect to the database, such as the MySQL ODBC driver installed on the previous page.

1. Launch the program then select Execute SQL from the main File menu – this opens the Execute SQL window.
2. Click the Data Sources button in the Execute SQL window – this opens the Choose Data Source window.
3. Select the ODBC driver appropriate for the type of database (eg: MySQL Databases) then click the OK button to close the Choose Data Source window.

*Microsoft Query tool is bundled with Excel. If you have Office but cannot find the Query program, open Excel then select Data | Import External Data | New Database Query and Excel should prompt you to install the Query tool.*

**Choose Data Source**

Databases

<New Data Source>
dBASE Files*
Excel Files*
MS Access Database*
MySQL Databases*

OK
Cancel
Browse...
Options...
Delete

4. If the ODBC driver's dialog box now appears, just click Cancel to close it, unless you want to change any of the Connection Parameter fields.
5. Now back in the Execute SQL window type an SQL query into the text field labelled SQL Statement.

**Execute SQL**

SQL statement:

```
show databases
```

Execute

Cancel

Open...

Save...

Procedures...

Data Sources... | MySQL Databases

Database:

test

6.	Click the Execute button to execute the query.
7.	The Execute SQL window closes and results of the query are shown in the main Microsoft Query window.

The screenshot below illustrates how Microsoft Query displays the results of an SQL query to show all databases – the mysql and test databases are included when MySQL is first installed.

**Query1**

| Database |
|----------|
| mysql |
| test |

Record: 1

# Summary

- The Structured Query Language (SQL) is the standard language for communicating with databases

- SQL is standardized by the American National Standards Institute (ANSI) and the International Standards Organization (ISO)

- Data can be stored in a database, or retrieved from a database, by making an SQL query

- SQL queries can be made from an integral client application, such as the MySQL monitor

- Third-party applications can be used to make SQL queries via an intermediate driver using Open DataBase Connectivity (ODBC)

- Server-side scripts can make SQL queries to provide dynamic content to the user

- Computer programs can be written to make SQL queries to a database in an Integrated Development Environment (IDE) – such as Microsoft's Visual Basic IDE

- MySQL is the world's most popular open-source DataBase Management System (DBMS), recognized for its speed and reliability

- There are versions of MySQL for all popular operating systems – including Windows, Linux, Solaris and OS2

- The Microsoft Query tool can execute SQL queries against the MySQL DBMS via a MyODBC driver

# Getting started with SQL

This chapter introduces SQL queries that can be used to reveal existing databases, create new databases and delete existing databases. It demonstrates how to execute those queries both directly in the MySQL monitor and via an SQL script file.

## Covers

## Chapter Two

# Introducing databases

Databases are simply convenient storage containers that store data in a structured manner. Every database is composed of one or more tables that structure the data into organized rows and columns. This makes it easy to reference and manipulate the data.

Each database table column has a label to identify the data stored within the table cells in that column. Each row contains an entry called a "record" that places data in each cell along that row.

A typical simple database table looks like this:

```
+-----------+-------+---------+----------+----------------+
| member_id | fname | lname   | tel      | email          |
+-----------+-------+---------+----------+----------------+
|         1 | John  | Smith   | 555-1234 | john@mail.com  |
|         2 | Ann   | Jones   | 555-5678 | anne@mail.com  |
|         3 | Mike  | McGrath | 555-3456 | mike@mail.com  |
+-----------+-------+---------+----------+----------------+
```

*Column label "member_id" features an underscore character because spaces are not allowed in labels.*

The rows of a database table are not automatically arranged in any particular order so they can be sorted alphabetically, numerically or by any other criteria. It is important, therefore, to have some means to identify each record in the table. The example above allocates a "member_id" for this purpose and this unique identifier is known as the **PRIMARY KEY**.

Storing data in a single table is very useful but relational databases with multiple tables introduce more possibilities by allowing the stored data to be combined in a variety of ways. For instance, the following two tables could be added to the database containing the first example table shown above:

```
+----------+-------------+          +-----------+----------+
| video_id | title       |          | member_id | video_id |
+----------+-------------+          +-----------+----------+
|        1 | Titanic     |          |         1 | 3        |
|        2 | Men In Black|          |         2 | 1        |
|        3 | Star Wars   |          |         3 | 2        |
+----------+-------------+          +-----------+----------+
```

The table on the left lists several video titles sorted numerically by "video_id" number. The table on the right describes a relationship between the tables that links each member to the video they have rented. So Anne (member #2) has Titanic (video #1), John (member #1) has Star Wars (video #3) and Mike (member #3) has Men In Black (video #2).

# Exploring databases

The SQL query that can be used to reveal all existing databases is:

```
SHOW DATABASES ;
```

Type this query at the prompt in the MySQL monitor to discover the names of all existing databases on your system.

*Terminate each SQL query with a semi-colon in the MySQL monitor.*

```
MySQL Command Line Client                    _ □ ×
mysql> SHOW DATABASES;
+-----------+
| Database  |
+-----------+
| mysql     |
| test      |
+-----------+
2 rows in set (0.00 sec)

mysql>
```

*SQL keywords are not case-sensitive but it is conventional to use uppercase characters for all SQL keywords..*

The MySQL installation creates two default databases. One is an empty database named "test" and another is named "mysql" that contains data which is used by the MySQL server itself.

In Linux start the MySQL monitor in a shell window with the command mysql -u root -p, and enter the root user password to ensure that you have full privileges, then use the SHOW DATABASES query to see all databases:

*Refer to the MySQL documentation for more on setting user privileges.*

```
Linux - Shell - Konsole
Session Edit View Bookmarks Settings Help
mysql> SHOW DATABASES;
+-----------+
| Database  |
+-----------+
| mysql     |
| test      |
+-----------+
2 rows in set (0.02 sec)

mysql>
```

# Creating a database

The SQL query to create a brand new database uses the SQL keywords **CREATE DATABASE** followed by a chosen name for that database, like this:

```
CREATE DATABASE database-name ;
```

So the SQL queries in the screenshots below create a new database called "library" – then confirm its existence.

*Database names may contain letters, digits and the underscore character – but they should not contain spaces or any other characters.*

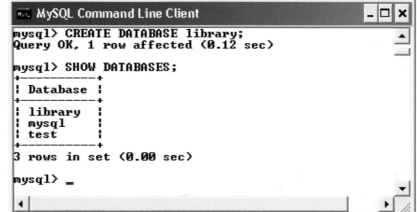

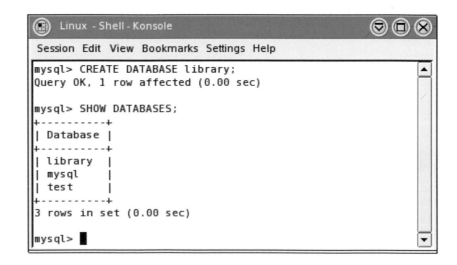

If an SQL query attempts to create a new database with the name of an existing database an error is reported. This can be avoided by qualifying the SQL query with the keywords IF NOT EXISTS so that it first checks to see if a database of that name already exists.

CREATE DATABASE IF NOT EXISTS *database-name* ;

In the screenshot below, the first SQL query attempts to create a new database called "library", which was already created in the previous example – so an error message is generated.

The second query is qualified to check that no database of that name already exists – so no error is generated.

In each case no new database is created and the existing "library" database is unaffected by these queries.

*Use only lowercase characters for all database names to avoid any confusion of case-sensitivity.*

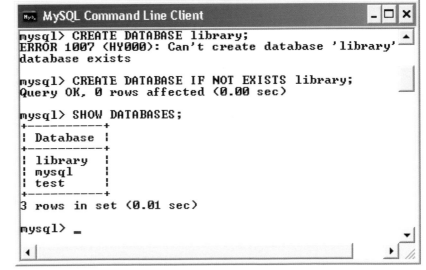

```
mysql> CREATE DATABASE library;
ERROR 1007 (HY000): Can't create database 'library'
database exists

mysql> CREATE DATABASE IF NOT EXISTS library;
Query OK, 0 rows affected (0.00 sec)

mysql> SHOW DATABASES;
+----------+
| Database |
+----------+
| library  |
| mysql    |
| test     |
+----------+
3 rows in set (0.01 sec)

mysql> _
```

In MySQL database names are case-sensitive on operating systems that have case-sensitive file names, such as Linux. So MySQL on Linux regards databases "LIBRARY" and "library" as two different databases. Windows, however, makes no case-sensitive distinction so would regard "LIBRARY" and "library" as the same database.

# Deleting a database

The SQL query to delete an existing database uses the SQL keywords DROP DATABASE followed by its name, like this:

```
DROP DATABASE database-name ;
```

The first SQL query in the screenshot below confirms the existence of a database called "library", that was created in the previous example. The subsequent queries delete the "library" database then confirms that it no longer exists. Notice how multiple queries can be typed at the prompt then executed together.

```
MySQL Command Line Client
mysql> SHOW DATABASES;
+----------+
| Database |
+----------+
| library  |
| mysql    |
| test     |
+----------+
3 rows in set (0.00 sec)

mysql> DROP DATABASE library; SHOW DATABASES;
Query OK, 0 rows affected (0.03 sec)

+----------+
| Database |
+----------+
| mysql    |
| test     |
+----------+
2 rows in set (0.00 sec)

mysql> _
```

If an SQL query attempts to delete a database that does not already exist an error is reported. This can be avoided by qualifying the SQL query with the keywords IF EXISTS so that it first checks to see if a database of that name already exists.

```
DROP DATABASE IF EXISTS database-name ;
```

In the screenshot below, the SQL query first attempts to delete a database called "library", which was already deleted in the previous example – so an error message is generated.

The subsequent query is qualified to check that a database of that name already exists – so no error is generated.

```
MySQL Command Line Client

mysql> SHOW DATABASES;
+------------+
| Database   |
+------------+
| mysql      |
| test       |
+------------+
2 rows in set (0.00 sec)

mysql> DROP DATABASE library;
ERROR 1008 (HY000): Can't drop database 'library';
database doesn't exist

mysql> DROP DATABASE IF EXISTS library;
Query OK, 0 rows affected, 1 warning (0.00 sec)

mysql>
```

```
Linux - Shell - Konsole

Session  Edit  View  Bookmarks  Settings  Help

mysql> SHOW DATABASES;
+------------+
| Database   |
+------------+
| mysql      |
| test       |
+------------+
2 rows in set (0.00 sec)

mysql> DROP DATABASE library;
ERROR 1008 (HY000): Can't drop database 'library';
database doesn't exist

mysql> DROP DATABASE IF EXISTS library;
Query OK, 0 rows affected, 1 warning (0.00 sec)

mysql>
```

# Running SQL scripts in MySQL

A number of SQL queries can be created as an SQL script which can then be run by MySQL. The script is simply a plain text file with a ".sql" file extension.

*In Linux systems remember to give the /home/SQL directory full permissions.*

It's convenient to create a directory to store SQL scripts. The examples in the rest of this book use SQL scripts stored in a directory at C:\SQL on Windows systems and in a directory at /home/SQL on Linux systems.

SQL scripts are executed in the MySQL monitor by typing the word "source", followed by a space, then the full path to the script file.

*The MySQL "source" keyword can alternatively be replaced by "\".*

Comments can usefully be added to SQL scripts to explain the purpose of particular queries. This can make scripts more comprehensible to other people or when revisiting a script at a later date. Single-line comments begin with a "#" or with "--". Multi-line C-style comments begin with "/*" and end with "*/".

The SQL script listed below reveals all databases then creates a new database if one does not already exist with that chosen name. The final query in this script confirms that the new database has indeed been created by, once more, revealing all databases.

*create-db.sql*

```
# Reveal existing databases
SHOW DATABASES;

/*
   Create a new database called "my_database" only if
   a database does not already exist with that name
*/
CREATE DATABASE IF NOT EXISTS my_database;

-- Reveal all databases
SHOW DATABASES;
```

Running the above script in the MySQL monitor executes the queries just as if they had been typed at the prompt.

The screenshots on the opposite page illustrate that the new database called "my_database" has been created on both Windows and Linux systems.

The rest of this book uses the my_database database created here to demonstrate features of SQL.

```
mysql> source C:\SQL\create-db.sql
+----------+
| Database |
+----------+
| mysql    |
| test     |
+----------+
2 rows in set (0.37 sec)

Query OK, 1 row affected (0.09 sec)

+-------------+
| Database    |
+-------------+
| my_database |
| mysql       |
| test        |
+-------------+
3 rows in set (0.00 sec)

mysql>
```

MySQL Command Line Client

```
mysql> source /home/SQL/create-db.sql
+----------+
| Database |
+----------+
| mysql    |
| test     |
+----------+
2 rows in set (0.00 sec)

Query OK, 1 row affected (0.02 sec)

+-------------+
| Database    |
+-------------+
| my_database |
| mysql       |
| test        |
+-------------+
3 rows in set (0.00 sec)

mysql>
```

Linux - Shell - Konsole
Session  Edit  View  Bookmarks  Settings  Help

# Summary

- Databases are containers that store data in a structured manner

- A database table stores data in organized rows and columns

- Each row in a database table is known as a "record"

- A PRIMARY KEY is a unique identifier for each record

- Relational databases allow data stored in multiple tables to be combined in a variety of ways

- The SHOW DATABASES query reveals all databases

- Each SQL query should end with a semi-colon

- The CREATE DATABASE query can be used to create a new database of a specified name

- The CREATE DATABASE query can be qualified with IF NOT EXISTS to ensure a database does not already exist of that name

- The DROP DATABASE query deletes a specified database

- The DROP DATABASE query can be qualified with IF EXISTS to ensure that a database does exist of that specified name

- An SQL script file is a plain text file with a ".sql" file extension

- SQL queries can be typed directly into the MySQL monitor or written in a SQL script file then run by MySQL

- Comments can be added to an SQL script to explain the purpose of specific queries

- Queries in an SQL script are executed by MySQL just as if they had been typed at the MySQL monitor prompt

# Creating database tables

This chapter introduces database tables where data is stored in rows and columns. Examples demonstrate how to create a table, how to specify the type of data each field may contain and how to restrict the field data with modifiers.

## Covers

**Chapter Three**

# Exploring database tables

To work with any database it is necessary to first tell MySQL which database to use with this SQL query:

```
USE database-name ;
```

Once the database has been selected it is possible to view a list of all the tables it contains with this SQL query:

```
SHOW TABLES ;
```

The SQL script below contains queries to select the default "mysql" database and list all the tables it contains.

*show-tbl.sql*

```
# Use the default MySQL database
USE mysql;

# List the MySQL database tables
SHOW TABLES;
```

```
MySQL Command Line Client                          _ □ ×
mysql> source C:\SQL\show-tbl.sql
Database changed
+----------------------------+
| Tables_in_mysql            |
+----------------------------+
| columns_priv               |
| db                         |
| func                       |
| help_category              |
| help_keyword               |
| help_relation              |
| help_topic                 |
| host                       |
| tables_priv                |
| time_zone                  |
| time_zone_leap_second      |
| time_zone_name             |
| time_zone_transition       |
| time_zone_transition_type  |
| user                       |
+----------------------------+
15 rows in set (0.05 sec)

mysql> _
```

In order to examine any table format its column specifications can be revealed with this SQL query:

```
EXPLAIN table-name ;
```

This query does not reveal any data contained within the table but lists the name of each table column together with details of the type of data they may contain and any restrictions that have been placed upon them.

The SQL script listed below examines the table named "db" within the default "mysql" database.

*explain-tbl.sql*

```
# Use the default MySQL database
USE mysql;

# Examine the "db" table
EXPLAIN db;
```

*It is not important to understand the table format in the example – this simply demonstrates that table formats can be examined with the SQL EXPLAIN keyword.*

```
MySQL Command Line Client                            _ □ ✕

mysql> source C:\SQL\explain-tbl.sql
Database changed
+-----------------------+------------------+------+-----
| Field                 | Type             | Null | Ke
+-----------------------+------------------+------+-----
| Host                  | char(60)         |      | PR
| Db                    | char(64)         |      | PR
| User                  | char(16)         |      | PR
| Select_priv           | enum('N','Y')    |      |
| Insert_priv           | enum('N','Y')    |      |
| Update_priv           | enum('N','Y')    |      |
| Delete_priv           | enum('N','Y')    |      |
| Create_priv           | enum('N','Y')    |      |
| Drop_priv             | enum('N','Y')    |      |
| Grant_priv            | enum('N','Y')    |      |
| References_priv       | enum('N','Y')    |      |
| Index_priv            | enum('N','Y')    |      |
| Alter_priv            | enum('N','Y')    |      |
| Create_tmp_table_priv | enum('N','Y')    |      |
| Lock_tables_priv      | enum('N','Y')    |      |
+-----------------------+------------------+------+-----
15 rows in set (0.02 sec)

mysql> _
```

# Creating a table

A new table can be created in a database using this query:

```
CREATE TABLE table-name ;
```

This type of query can be qualified with IF NOT EXISTS to ensure that a table of the specified name does not already exist:

```
CREATE TABLE IF NOT EXISTS table-name ;
```

*A comprehensive table of all SQL data type keywords appears on page 38.*

The SQL statement in this query must be followed by parentheses defining the name of each column and the type of data that it may contain. Each column definition is separated from the next by a comma.

The SQL script listed below uses the database named "my_database" that was created in the previous chapter. It creates a table named "fruit" within that database.

The "fruit" table contains three columns named "id", "name" and "color". The INT SQL keyword specifies that the "id" column may only contain integer values. The TEXT keyword specifies that the "name" and "color" columns may only contain text values.

*create-tbl.sql*
*(part of)*

```
# List all databases
SHOW DATABASES ;

# Use the "my_database" database
USE my_database ;

# create a table called "fruit" with 3 columns
CREATE TABLE IF NOT EXISTS fruit
(
    id       INT,
    name     TEXT,
    color    TEXT
) ;
```

*Notice how the CREATE TABLE query formats the column definitions for better readability – additional spaces and line breaks are ignored.*

*create-tbl.sql*
*(cont'd)*

```
# show that the table has been created
SHOW TABLES;

# confirm the "fruit" table format
EXPLAIN fruit;
```

```
■ MySQL Command Line Client                          _ □ ✕

mysql> \. C:\SQL\create-tbl.sql
+--------------+
¦ Database     ¦
+--------------+
¦ my_database  ¦
¦ mysql        ¦
¦ test         ¦
+--------------+
3 rows in set (0.03 sec)

Database changed
Query OK, 0 rows affected (0.89 sec)

+-----------------------+
¦ Tables_in_my_database ¦
+-----------------------+
¦ fruit                 ¦
+-----------------------+
1 row in set (0.00 sec)

+-------+---------+------+-----+---------+-------+
¦ Field ¦ Type    ¦ Null ¦ Key ¦ Default ¦ Extra ¦
+-------+---------+------+-----+---------+-------+
¦ id    ¦ int(11) ¦ YES  ¦     ¦ NULL    ¦       ¦
¦ name  ¦ text    ¦ YES  ¦     ¦ NULL    ¦       ¦
¦ color ¦ text    ¦ YES  ¦     ¦ NULL    ¦       ¦
+-------+---------+------+-----+---------+-------+
3 rows in set (0.01 sec)

mysql> _
```

*The precise format for database tables does vary in other DBMS' – check the documentation for your version.*

The EXPLAIN query reveals the format of the "fruit" table which allows the "id" field to contain integers up to 11 digits long – in actuality this is limited to values between the range of -2147483648 to 2147483647.

In this example "YES" denotes that each field is allowed to contain no value, defined by the NULL keyword. Each field has, in fact, been created with no default value, so does contain a NULL value. Note that NULL represents absolutely no value – this is not the same as an empty string that is represented by "".

# Deleting a table

A new table can be deleted from a database using this query:

> DROP TABLE *table-name* ;

This type of query can be qualified with IF EXISTS to ensure that a table of the specified name does already exist:

> DROP TABLE IF EXISTS *table-name* ;

When this query is executed no confirmation is sought – the table is immediately deleted along with any data that it contains.

The SQL script listed below uses the database named "my_database" that was created in the previous chapter. It creates a table named "dogs" containing two columns named "id" and "breed". After confirming that the "dogs" table has been created the script deletes that table along with the "fruit" table that was created in the previous example.

*delete-tbl.sql*

```
# Use the "my_database" database
USE my_database;

# create a table called "dogs" with 2 columns
CREATE TABLE IF NOT EXISTS dogs
(
   id        INT,
   breed     TEXT
);

# show that the table has been created
SHOW TABLES;

# confirm the "dogs" table format
EXPLAIN dogs;

# delete the "dogs" and "fruit" tables
DROP TABLE IF EXISTS dogs;
DROP TABLE IF EXISTS fruit;
```

This example creates the "dogs" table in the "my_database" database alongside the existing "fruits" table. Both tables are then deleted using two DROP TABLE queries.

The deletion of both tables can be accomplished with a single DROP TABLE query by stating the table names separated by a comma.

In this case the DROP TABLE queries in the example code would be replaced by this single query:

```
# delete the "dogs" and "fruit" tables
DROP TABLE IF EXISTS dogs, fruit;
```

Multiple tables can be deleted using this technique – but the deletion is permanent and there is no "undo" facility.

# Table data types

The table below describes the range of data type specifiers that can be used when defining database table columns. It is advisable to specify the permitted data type precisely. For instance, if a column only contains short strings use VARCHAR() rather than TEXT.

| | |
|---|---|
| INT | An integer from -2,147,483,648 to 2,147,483,647 |
| DECIMAL | A floating point number that can specify the number of permissable digits. For example DECIMAL(3,2) permits -999.99 to 999.99 |
| DOUBLE | A long double-precision floating point number |
| DATE | A date in the YYY-MM-DD format |
| TIME | A time in the HH:MM:SS format |
| DATETIME | A combined date and time in the format YYY-MM-DD HH:MM:SS |
| YEAR | A year 1901-2155 in either YY or YYYY format |
| TIMESTAMP | Automatic date and time of last record entry |
| CHAR() | A string of defined <u>fixed</u> length up to 255 characters long. For example, CHAR(100) pads a smaller string to make it 100 characters long |
| VARCHAR() | A string of <u>variable</u> length up to 255 characters long that is stored without padding |
| TEXT | A string up to 65,535 characters long |
| BLOB | A binary type for variable data |
| ENUM | A single string value from a defined list. For example, ENUM("red", "green", "blue") allows entry of any one of these three colors only |
| SET | A string or multiple strings from a defined list. For example, SET("red", "green", "blue") allows entry of any one, or more, of these colors |

The SQL script, listed opposite, creates a table that includes data type specifiers in the column definitions. The "id" column only accepts integer values. The date and time of each entry is automatically recorded in the "date" column. The "first_name" and "last_name" columns may each contain up to 20 characters.

*data-types.sql*

```
# Use the "my_database" database
USE my_database;

# create a table called "user_log" with 3 columns
CREATE TABLE IF NOT EXISTS user_log
(
    id              INT,
    date            TIMESTAMP,
    first_name      VARCHAR(20),
    last_name       VARCHAR(20)
);

# confirm the "user_log" table format
EXPLAIN user_log;

# delete this sample table
DROP TABLE user_log;
```

```
MySQL Command Line Client                          _ □ ×

mysql> source C:\SQL\data-types.sql
Database changed
Query OK, 0 rows affected (0.12 sec)

+------------+-------------+------+-----+-----------+
| Field      | Type        | Null | Key | Default   |
+------------+-------------+------+-----+-----------+
| id         | int(11)     | YES  |     | NULL      |
| date       | timestamp   | YES  |     | CURRENT_T |
| first_name | varchar(20) | YES  |     | NULL      |
| last_name  | varchar(20) | YES  |     | NULL      |
+------------+-------------+------+-----+-----------+
4 rows in set (0.00 sec)

Query OK, 0 rows affected (0.04 sec)

mysql> _
```

After the EXPLAIN query confirms the column definitions this sample table is deleted by a DROP TABLE query. Many examples in this book follow the same procedure in order to make the examples self-contained, without accumulating a large number of example tables in the "my_database" database.

# Table field modifiers

In addition to specifying permissible data types, with the keywords on the previous page, the modifier keywords in the following table can optionally be used to further control column content:

| | |
|---|---|
| NOT NULL | Insists that each record must include a data value in this column |
| UNIQUE | Insists that records may not duplicate any entry in this column |
| AUTO_INCREMENT | Available only for numeric columns, to automatically generate a number that is one more than the previous value in that column |
| DEFAULT | Specifies a value to be used where no value is stated for this column when a record is inserted |
| PRIMARY KEY | Specifies the column, or columns, to be used as the primary key for that table |

*The PRIMARY KEY modifier is described on page 42.*

When it is essential that a record must include a value for a column, that column should be defined with the NOT NULL modifier. This allows an empty string "" to be stored there but does not allow that column to be empty or NULL.

When the data stored in a column should never be duplicated that column should be defined with the UNIQUE modifier. For instance, to avoid the accidental duplication of product codes.

The AUTO_INCREMENT modifier is particularly useful to automatically generate incremental identity numbers for each row – the first row will be numbered 1, the second row 2, and so on.

Setting a column DEFAULT allows records to be inserted without tediously requiring a value for a column that is usually constant. For instance, a "quantity" column might usually contain a value of 1 in each record – so 1 could be set as its default value.

The SQL script listed below creates a table that uses modifiers in its column definitions to control the permissible content. The "id" column automatically numbers each row and the "qty" column will contain 1 unless another value is inserted. All the other columns must contain data values – they can't be empty or NULL.

*modifiers.sql*

```
# Use the "my_database" database
USE my_database;

# create a table called "products" with 5 columns
CREATE TABLE IF NOT EXISTS products
(
   id        INT          UNIQUE AUTO_INCREMENT,
   code      INT          NOT NULL,
   name      VARCHAR(25)  NOT NULL,
   qty       INT          DEFAULT 1,
   price     DECIMAL(6,2) NOT NULL
);

# confirm the "products" table format
EXPLAIN products;

# delete this sample table
DROP TABLE products;
```

*The right-hand column in this illustration is headed "Extras" and notes the "auto_increment" modifier.*

```
 MySQL Command Line Client                          _ □ ×
mysql> source C:\SQL\modifiers.sql
Database changed
Query OK, 0 rows affected (0.09 sec)

+-------+-------------+------+-----+---------+------+
| Field | Type        | Null | Key | Default | Ext  |
+-------+-------------+------+-----+---------+------+
| id    | int(11)     |      | PRI | NULL    | aut  |
| code  | int(11)     |      |     | 0       |      |
| name  | varchar(25) |      |     |         |      |
| qty   | int(11)     | YES  |     | 1       |      |
| price | decimal(6,2)|      |     | 0.00    |      |
+-------+-------------+------+-----+---------+------+
5 rows in set (0.01 sec)

Query OK, 0 rows affected (0.04 sec)

mysql> _
```

# Setting the primary key

A PRIMARY KEY is a "constraint" that is applied to a column to uniquely identify each row of that database table. It ensures that the values in each row of that column are unique and never change, so those values can be used to reference any specific row.

By setting the PRIMARY KEY constraint it is possible to manipulate data on specific rows of the database table.

Any column can be set as the PRIMARY KEY but is often the first column that is used to provide a unique identifying number.

Any column set as the PRIMARY KEY must meet these criteria:

- Each field in that column must have a value – it may not be empty or have a NULL value

- Each value in that column must be unique – there must be no duplications

- Each value in that column can never be modified or updated

- Each value in that column cannot be re-used – when a row is deleted its PRIMARY KEY value cannot be re-assigned as the PRIMARY KEY value of a new row

Notice in the previous example that MySQL automatically set the "id" column as the PRIMARY KEY because of the UNIQUE modifier that was included in that column's definition. This is indicated in the output from the EXPLAIN query, on page 41, by the term "PRI" listed under the "Key" heading. This is logical because any column that may only contain unique values can be used to identify each table row by that column's value.

The PRIMARY KEY constraint can be set by adding the PRIMARY KEY keywords to the column definition in the CREATE TABLE query. Alternatively a PRIMARY KEY can be set elsewhere in the CREATE TABLE query by stating the name of the column in parentheses after the PRIMARY KEY keywords.

The SQL script on the opposite page creates two tables with a PRIMARY KEY column set by different methods. Each table can reference any specific row by its "id" value. Notice that the EXPLAIN queries confirm both PRIMARY KEY settings.

*primary-key.sql*

```sql
# Use the "my_database" database
USE my_database;

# create a table called "cups" with 2 columns
CREATE TABLE IF NOT EXISTS cups
(
  id              INT    AUTO_INCREMENT PRIMARY KEY,
  cup_pattern     VARCHAR(25)
);

# create a table called "saucers" with 2 columns
CREATE TABLE IF NOT EXISTS saucers
(
  id              INT    AUTO_INCREMENT,
  scr_pattern     VARCHAR(25),
  PRIMARY KEY(id)
);

# confirm the "cups" and "saucers" table format
EXPLAIN cups; EXPLAIN saucers;

# delete these sample tables
DROP TABLE cups, saucers;
```

```
 MySQL Command Line Client                            _ □ ✕

mysql> source C:\SQL\primary-key.sql
Database changed
Query OK, 0 rows affected (0.53 sec)

Query OK, 0 rows affected (0.11 sec)

+-------------+-------------+------+-----+---------+
| Field       | Type        | Null | Key | Default |
+-------------+-------------+------+-----+---------+
| id          | int(11)     |      | PRI | NULL    |
| cup_pattern | varchar(25) | YES  |     | NULL    |
+-------------+-------------+------+-----+---------+
2 rows in set (0.00 sec)

+-------------+-------------+------+-----+---------+
| Field       | Type        | Null | Key | Default |
+-------------+-------------+------+-----+---------+
| id          | int(11)     |      | PRI | NULL    |
| scr_pattern | varchar(25) | YES  |     | NULL    |
+-------------+-------------+------+-----+---------+
2 rows in set (0.00 sec)

Query OK, 0 rows affected (0.07 sec)
```

# Altering a table

The format of an existing database table can be changed with an ALTER TABLE query. This query can make a single alteration or specify a number of alterations as a comma-separated list.

The ALTER TABLE query is supported by all DBMS' but there are variations in its capability – you must check the documentation for your particular DBMS to discover other ALTER TABLE options.

An ALTER TABLE query can ADD a complete new COLUMN to an existing table, like this:

```
ALTER TABLE table-name
ADD COLUMN name data-type optional-modifier/s ;
```

It can also ADD a PRIMARY KEY to an existing column definition using this syntax:

```
ALTER TABLE table-name
ADD PRIMARY KEY( column-name ) ;
```

In the ADD COLUMN and DROP COLUMN examples the COLUMN keyword is optional – it is what the manual calls "a pure noise word" that is only available to aid readability.

An ALTER TABLE query can CHANGE the name of an existing column. The new column will not inherit any data type or modifiers specified to the original column – these must be set anew in the ALTER TABLE query, like this:

```
ALTER TABLE table-name
CHANGE old-column-name new-column-name
        date-type optional-modifier/s ;
```

An ALTER TABLE query can also permanently delete an entire column from the table using the DROP COLUMN keywords:

```
ALTER TABLE table-name
DROP COLUMN column-name ;
```

Care should be taken in using this technique as it will remove any data that is contained in that column – it cannot be recovered.

The SQL script on the opposite page demonstrates all of the possibilities described on this page.

*alter-tbl.sql*

```
USE my_database;    # Use the "my_database" database

# create a table called "dishes" with 3 columns
CREATE TABLE IF NOT EXISTS dishes
(
    id          INT          NOT NULL,
    pattern     VARCHAR(25)  NOT NULL,
    price       DECIMAL(6,2)
);

EXPLAIN dishes;     # confirm the "dishes" table format

# update the "dishes" table
ALTER TABLE dishes
    ADD PRIMARY KEY(id),
    ADD COLUMN code INT UNIQUE NOT NULL,
    CHANGE pattern dish_pattern VARCHAR(25) NOT NULL,
    DROP COLUMN price;

EXPLAIN dishes;     # confirm the "dishes" table format
DROP TABLE dishes;  # delete this sample table
```

*Altering tables that contain data can have unpredictable results and should really be avoided.*

*Well designed database tables should never need to be altered if they anticipate all likely future requirements.*

**MySQL Command Line Client**

```
mysql> source C:\SQL\alter-tbl.sql
Database changed
Query OK, 0 rows affected (0.09 sec)

+---------+--------------+------+-----+---------+---+
| Field   | Type         | Null | Key | Default | E |
+---------+--------------+------+-----+---------+---+
| id      | int(11)      |      |     | 0       |   |
| pattern | varchar(25)  |      |     |         |   |
| price   | decimal(6,2) | YES  |     | NULL    |   |
+---------+--------------+------+-----+---------+---+
3 rows in set (0.00 sec)

Query OK, 0 rows affected (0.34 sec)
Records: 0  Duplicates: 0  Warnings: 0

+--------------+-------------+------+-----+---------+
| Field        | Type        | Null | Key | Default |
+--------------+-------------+------+-----+---------+
| id           | int(11)     |      | PRI | 0       |
| dish_pattern | varchar(25) |      |     |         |
| code         | int(11)     |      | UNI | 0       |
+--------------+-------------+------+-----+---------+
3 rows in set (0.00 sec)

Query OK, 0 rows affected (0.04 sec)
```

# Summary

- The USE DATABASE query selects a database to work with

- The names of all the tables in a database can be revealed with the SHOW TABLES query

- The format of a table can be examined with an EXPLAIN query

- A new table can be created with the CREATE TABLE query

- The CREATE TABLE query can be qualified with IF NOT EXISTS to ensure that a table of the specified name does not already exist

- An existing table can be deleted with a DROP TABLE query

- The DROP TABLE query can be qualified with IF EXISTS to ensure that a table of the specified name already exists

- A column definition should specify the data type that it may contain using recognized data type keywords such as INT, DOUBLE, DECIMAL, DATETIME, TIMESTAMP, DATE, TIME, YEAR, CHAR(), VARCHAR(), TEXT, BLOB, ENUM or SET

- Optionally, a column definition may specify a field modifier to further control that column's permissible content to make it NOT NULL, AUTO_INCREMENT, UNIQUE, DEFAULT or PRIMARY KEY

- When a column is set as a PRIMARY KEY each row must contain unique unalterable data in that column which can be used to identify each row of that table

- An ALTER TABLE query can be used to ADD a new column to an existing table

- An ALTER TABLE query can be used to CHANGE a column in an existing table

- An ALTER TABLE query can be used to delete a column from an existing table with the DROP keyword

- Attempting to alter tables that contain data may have unpredictable results and is not recommended

- Well-designed database tables should never need to be altered

# Inserting data into tables

This chapter demonstrates how to insert data into database tables. Examples show how to insert both complete rows of data and just partial rows. It also illustrates how to update and delete existing data within a database table.

## Covers

**Chapter Four**

# Inserting complete rows

Data can be inserted into an existing database table with an INSERT INTO query that first specifies the table name. The SQL VALUES keyword then specifies the actual data to be inserted as a comma-separated list within parentheses, like this:

```
INSERT INTO table-name VALUES ( value, value ) ;
```

Any text values must be enclosed within quotes.

Each INSERT INTO query inserts just one row into the database table. A data value must be specified for each column – and in the corresponding order. The data to be inserted must also match the data type in each column's definition or an error will be generated. The NULL keyword can be specified to leave a field empty if that column's definition allows NULL values. All data contained in a table can be displayed with a SELECT query using the ★ wildcard and the FROM keyword like this:

```
SELECT * FROM table-name ;
```

The following SQL script first creates a table named "prints" with 3 columns. Three complete rows of data are then inserted into the table by individual INSERT INTO queries. This is confirmed by a SELECT query that displays all the data within that table.

*insert-data.sql*
*(part of)*

```
# use the "my_database" database
USE my_database;

# create a table named "prints" with 3 columns
CREATE TABLE prints
(
    id          INT             NOT NULL,
    code        VARCHAR(8)      NOT NULL,
    name        VARCHAR(20)     NOT NULL,
    PRIMARY KEY(id)
);
```

*insert-data.sql*
*(cont'd)*

```
# now insert 3 records into the "prints" table
INSERT INTO prints VALUES
(
  1, "624/1636", "Lower Manhattan"
);

INSERT INTO prints VALUES
(
  2, "624/1904", "Hill Town"
);

INSERT INTO prints VALUES
(
  3, "624/1681", "Roscoff Trawlers"
);

# show all data in the "prints" table
SELECT * FROM prints;

# delete this sample table
DROP TABLE prints;
```

The "code" column definition allows VARCHAR data rather than INT data to allow for the "/" slash character that appears in these code numbers.

If the table columns get altered, the listed data values may not match the column definitions so an error will be generated – the example on the next page demonstrates how this can be avoided.

```
Linux - Shell - Konsole
Session  Edit  View  Bookmarks  Settings  Help

mysql> source /home/SQL/insert-data.sql
Database changed
Query OK, 0 rows affected (0.03 sec)

Query OK, 1 row affected (0.00 sec)

Query OK, 1 row affected (0.00 sec)

Query OK, 1 row affected (0.00 sec)

+----+----------+------------------+
| id | code     | name             |
+----+----------+------------------+
|  1 | 624/1636 | Lower Manhattan  |
|  2 | 624/1904 | Hill Town        |
|  3 | 624/1681 | Roscoff Trawlers |
+----+----------+------------------+
3 rows in set (0.00 sec)

Query OK, 0 rows affected (0.01 sec)
```

# Including a columns list

The INSERT INTO query, introduced in the previous example, can be improved by adding a "columns list" to explicitly specify the table column into which each value should be inserted. This changes the syntax of the INSERT INTO query to look like this:

```
INSERT INTO table-name ( column, column )
VALUES ( value, value ) ;
```

When the INSERT INTO query contains a columns list the DBMS matches each value to the specified column in the order in which they are listed – the value listed first will be matched to the column listed first, the value listed second will be matched to the column listed second, and so on.

The number of listed values must match the number of listed columns, but the columns need not be listed in the order in which they appear in the database table.

Additionally a columns list need not list all the columns in the table providing that omitted columns allow NULL values. This allows an INSERT INTO query to insert only partial rows.

*Always include a columns list in each INSERT INTO query to prevent possible future database problems.*

It is strongly recommended that all INSERT INTO queries should include a columns list so that the query may remain valid in the event that the table gets altered.

The SQL script on the opposite page first creates a table then inserts three records, each using a columns list.

The columns list in the first INSERT INTO query lists all the columns in the same order in which they appear in the table.

The columns list in the second INSERT INTO query again lists all the columns but in a different order to that in which they appear in the table. The values are listed in an order corresponding to this columns list.

The columns list in the third INSERT INTO query lists only the first two columns in the table – the value for the third column is provided by the default specified in the column definition.

*cols-list.sql*

```
# use the "my_database" database
USE my_database;

# create a table named "towels" with 3 columns
CREATE TABLE towels
(
    code        VARCHAR(8)     NOT NULL PRIMARY KEY,
    name        VARCHAR(20)    NOT NULL,
    color       VARCHAR(20)    DEFAULT "White"
);

# insert 3 records into the "towels" table
INSERT INTO towels ( code, name, color )
VALUES ( "821/7355", "Dolphin", "Blue" );

INSERT INTO towels ( color, code, name )
VALUES ( "Lilac", "830/1921", "Daisy" );

INSERT INTO towels ( code, name )
VALUES ( "830/2078", "Starburst" );

# show all "towels" data
SELECT * FROM towels;
```

*The "towels" table created in this example is not deleted by this script - the table is used by other examples in this chapter.*

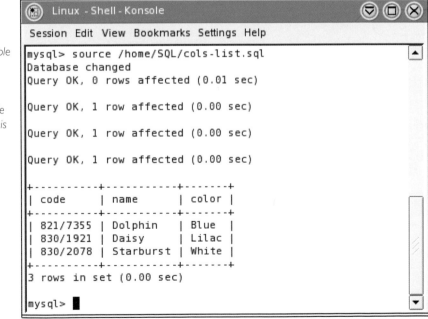

```
Linux - Shell - Konsole
Session  Edit  View  Bookmarks  Settings  Help
mysql> source /home/SQL/cols-list.sql
Database changed
Query OK, 0 rows affected (0.01 sec)

Query OK, 1 row affected (0.00 sec)

Query OK, 1 row affected (0.00 sec)

Query OK, 1 row affected (0.00 sec)

+----------+-----------+-------+
| code     | name      | color |
+----------+-----------+-------+
| 821/7355 | Dolphin   | Blue  |
| 830/1921 | Daisy     | Lilac |
| 830/2078 | Starburst | White |
+----------+-----------+-------+
3 rows in set (0.00 sec)

mysql>
```

# Inserting selected data

Data can be inserted into a table from another table with an INSERT SELECT query using this syntax:

```
INSERT INTO destination-table ( column, column )
SELECT * FROM source-table ;
```

This example copies all the records from the "towels" table, created in the previous example, into the "bath_towels" table.

*insert-select.sql*

```
# use the "my_database" database
USE my_database;

# create a table named "bath_towels" with 3 columns
CREATE TABLE bath_towels
(
    code        VARCHAR(8)      NOT NULL PRIMARY KEY,
    name        VARCHAR(20)     NOT NULL,
    color       VARCHAR(20)     DEFAULT "White"
);
```

*In this example both tables have identically-named columns. This is not essential but the data types must match.*

```
# insert 2 records into the "bath_towels" table
INSERT INTO bath_towels ( code, name, color )
VALUES ( "821/9735", "Harvest", "Beige" );

INSERT INTO bath_towels ( code, name, color )
VALUES ( "821/9628", "Wine", "Maroon" );

# show all tables in the "my_database" database
SHOW TABLES;
```

*The SELECT query returns the value of each field on each row of the source table. These are copied, in order, into the fields of the destination table specified in the columns list.*

```
# show all "bath_towels" and "towels" data
SELECT * FROM bath_towels;
SELECT * FROM towels;

# add the "towels" data to the "bath_towels" table
INSERT INTO bath_towels ( code, name, color )
SELECT * FROM towels;

# show all "bath_towels" data
SELECT * FROM bath_towels;
```

```
┌──────────────────────────────────────────────────────────────────────┐
│ (⚙)  Linux - Shell - Konsole                          (⧩)(⬜)(⊗)      │
├──────────────────────────────────────────────────────────────────────┤
│  Session  Edit  View  Bookmarks  Settings  Help                        │
├──────────────────────────────────────────────────────────────────────┤
│ mysql> source /home/SQL/insert-select.sql                          ▲  │
│ Database changed                                                      │
│ Query OK, 0 rows affected (0.02 sec)                                  │
│                                                                       │
│ Query OK, 1 row affected (0.00 sec)                                   │
│                                                                       │
│ Query OK, 1 row affected (0.00 sec)                                   │
│                                                                       │
│ +-----------------------+                                             │
│ | Tables_in_my_database |                                             │
│ +-----------------------+                                             │
│ | bath_towels           |                                             │
│ | towels                |                                             │
│ +-----------------------+                                             │
│ 2 rows in set (0.00 sec)                                              │
│                                                                       │
│ +----------+---------+--------+                                       │
│ | code     | name    | color  |                                      │
│ +----------+---------+--------+                                       │
│ | 821/9735 | Harvest | Beige  |                                      │
│ | 821/9628 | Wine    | Maroon |                                      │
│ +----------+---------+--------+                                       │
│ 2 rows in set (0.00 sec)                                              │
│                                                                       │
│ +----------+-----------+--------+                                     │
│ | code     | name      | color  |                                    │
│ +----------+-----------+--------+                                     │
│ | 821/7355 | Dolphin   | Blue   |                                    │
│ | 830/1921 | Daisy     | Lilac  |                                    │
│ | 830/2078 | Starburst | White  |                                    │
│ +----------+-----------+--------+                                     │
│ 3 rows in set (0.00 sec)                                              │
│                                                                       │
│ Query OK, 3 rows affected (0.01 sec)                                  │
│ Records: 3  Duplicates: 0  Warnings: 0                                │
│                                                                       │
│ +----------+-----------+--------+                                     │
│ | code     | name      | color  |                                    │
│ +----------+-----------+--------+                                     │
│ | 821/9735 | Harvest   | Beige  |                                    │
│ | 821/9628 | Wine      | Maroon |                                    │
│ | 821/7355 | Dolphin   | Blue   |                                    │
│ | 830/1921 | Daisy     | Lilac  |                                    │
│ | 830/2078 | Starburst | White  |                                    │
│ +----------+-----------+--------+                                     │
│ 5 rows in set (0.00 sec)                                           ▼  │
└──────────────────────────────────────────────────────────────────────┘
```

*An INSERT query only inserts a single record. Multiple INSERT queries must be used to insert multiple records. An INSERT SELECT query, on the other hand, copies all the records from the source table.*

# Updating data

All the data contained within a column of a database table can be changed with an UPDATE query, that has this syntax:

> UPDATE *table-name* SET *column-name* = *value* ;

The UPDATE keyword is followed by the name of the table to work with and the SET keyword specifies the name of the column to be updated with a new specified value.

Note that this SQL query will update every field in the specified column with the single specified value.

In the SQL script listed below, the "bath_towels" table, created in the previous example, is updated so that all the fields in its "color" column are set to "White".

*update-all.sql*

```
# use the "my_database" database
USE my_database;

# show all "bath_towels" data
SELECT * FROM bath_towels;

# update all fields in the "color" column
UPDATE bath_towels SET color = "White";

# show all "bath_towels" data
SELECT * FROM bath_towels;
```

The screenshot on the opposite page shows the "bath_towels" table both before and after the update has been performed as the result of executing the SQL script above.

In reality it is not often that all the fields in a column are required to be changed to the same single value – it's more likely that only specific fields are needed to be updated.

The example on page 56/57 shows how to identify specific column fields to be updated independently without affecting any other fields in that column.

```
Linux - Shell - Konsole

Session  Edit  View  Bookmarks  Settings  Help

mysql> source /home/SQL/update-all.sql
Database changed
+----------+-----------+--------+
| code     | name      | color  |
+----------+-----------+--------+
| 821/9735 | Harvest   | Beige  |
| 821/9628 | Wine      | Maroon |
| 821/7355 | Dolphin   | Blue   |
| 830/1921 | Daisy     | Lilac  |
| 830/2078 | Starburst | White  |
+----------+-----------+--------+
5 rows in set (0.01 sec)

Query OK, 4 rows affected (0.00 sec)
Rows matched: 5  Changed: 4  Warnings: 0

+----------+-----------+--------+
| code     | name      | color  |
+----------+-----------+--------+
| 821/9735 | Harvest   | White  |
| 821/9628 | Wine      | White  |
| 821/7355 | Dolphin   | White  |
| 830/1921 | Daisy     | White  |
| 830/2078 | Starburst | White  |
+----------+-----------+--------+
5 rows in set (0.00 sec)

mysql>
```

It is sometimes useful to remove all the values in a particular column using an UPDATE query to set each field to NULL – providing that the column definition allows NULL values.

# Changing specific data

Usually an **UPDATE** query will be required to change data contained in a particular field of a column on a specific row. The row can be identified by adding the **WHERE** keyword to the **UPDATE** query to match a value in a specified column. The syntax of the specific **UPDATE** query now looks like this:

```
UPDATE table-name SET column-name = value
WHERE column-name = value ;
```

A single **UPDATE** query can also change multiple column values on a specific row by making multiple column = value statements as a comma-delimited list after the **SET** keyword.

The SQL script listed below makes a number of **UPDATE** queries to the "bath_towels" table from the previous example. These change the values in the "color" column. The last **UPDATE** query changes the values of the "color" column and the "name" column on the row where the "code" column has the value "821/9628".

*update-where.sql*

```
# use the "my_database" database
USE my_database;

# show all "bath_towels" data
SELECT * FROM bath_towels;

# update specific fields in the "color" column
UPDATE bath_towels
SET color = "Beige" WHERE name = "Harvest";

UPDATE bath_towels
SET color = "Blue" WHERE name = "Dolphin";

UPDATE bath_towels
SET color = "Lilac" WHERE name = "Daisy";

UPDATE bath_towels
SET name = "Tempest", color = "Maroon"
WHERE code = "821/9628";

# show all "bath_towels" data
SELECT * FROM bath_towels;
```

```
┌─────────────────────────────────────────────────────────────────┐
│ (◉)  Linux - Shell - Konsole                      (▽)(□)(✕)       │
├─────────────────────────────────────────────────────────────────┤
│ Session  Edit  View  Bookmarks  Settings  Help                  │
├─────────────────────────────────────────────────────────────────┤
│ mysql> source /home/SQL/update-where.sql              ▲         │
│ Database changed                                                │
│ +----------+-----------+-------+                                │
│ | code     | name      | color |                                │
│ +----------+-----------+-------+                                │
│ | 821/9735 | Harvest   | White |                                │
│ | 821/9628 | Wine      | White |                                │
│ | 821/7355 | Dolphin   | White |                                │
│ | 830/1921 | Daisy     | White |                                │
│ | 830/2078 | Starburst | White |                                │
│ +----------+-----------+-------+                                │
│ 5 rows in set (0.00 sec)                                        │
│                                                                 │
│ Query OK, 1 row affected (0.00 sec)                             │
│ Rows matched: 1  Changed: 1  Warnings: 0                        │
│                                                                 │
│ Query OK, 1 row affected (0.00 sec)                             │
│ Rows matched: 1  Changed: 1  Warnings: 0                        │
│                                                                 │
│ Query OK, 1 row affected (0.00 sec)                             │
│ Rows matched: 1  Changed: 1  Warnings: 0                        │
│                                                                 │
│ Query OK, 1 row affected (0.01 sec)                             │
│ Rows matched: 1  Changed: 1  Warnings: 0                        │
│                                                                 │
│ +----------+-----------+--------+                               │
│ | code     | name      | color  |                              │
│ +----------+-----------+--------+                               │
│ | 821/9735 | Harvest   | Beige  |                              │
│ | 821/9628 | Tempest   | Maroon |                              │
│ | 821/7355 | Dolphin   | Blue   |                              │
│ | 830/1921 | Daisy     | Lilac  |                              │
│ | 830/2078 | Starburst | White  |                              │
│ +----------+-----------+--------+                               │
│ 5 rows in set (0.00 sec)                                        │
│                                                                 │
│ mysql> █                                             ▼          │
└─────────────────────────────────────────────────────────────────┘
```

*If the WHERE part of an UPDATE query is omitted the query will update all rows – lost data cannot be recovered.*

*Always use the table's PRIMARY KEY value to identify a row.*

In this example the **WHERE** keyword identifies rows by their "name" values in the first three **UPDATE** queries. This means that multiple rows could accidentally be updated if the "name" field on several rows contained identical values.

The final **UPDATE** query more correctly identifies the row by its **PRIMARY KEY** value in the "code" column – this is guaranteed to be unique so multiple rows cannot be accidentally updated.

# Deleting data

Rows can be removed from a database table with a DELETE query. All rows can be removed with this syntax:

> DELETE FROM *table-name* ;

More usually a specific row can be removed from a table by adding the WHERE keyword to a DELETE query to identify the row. The syntax of the DELETE query now looks like this:

> DELETE FROM *table-name* WHERE *column = value* ;

Two DELETE queries in the following SQL script first delete two specific rows of the "bath_towels" table from the previous example. A further DELETE query removes all the other rows then both the "bath_towels" and "towels" tables are deleted with DROP queries.

*delete-from.sql*

```
# use the "my_database" database
USE my_database;

# show all "bath_towels" data
SELECT * FROM bath_towels;

# delete two specific rows
DELETE FROM bath_towels WHERE code = "821/9735";
DELETE FROM bath_towels WHERE code = "821/7355";

# show all "bath_towels" data
SELECT * FROM bath_towels;

# delete all remaining rows in the "bath_towels" table
DELETE FROM bath_towels;

# show all "bath_towels" data
SELECT * FROM bath_towels;

# delete the "towels" and "bath_towels" tables
DROP TABLE towels;
DROP TABLE bath_towels;
```

*A DELETE query cannot delete the table itself – a DROP query is needed for that.*

```
┌────────────────────────────────────────────────────────┐
│ (✳) Linux - Shell - Konsole              ▽ ▢ ✕          │
├────────────────────────────────────────────────────────┤
│ Session Edit View Bookmarks Settings Help               │
├────────────────────────────────────────────────────────┤
│ mysql> source /home/SQL/delete-from.sql            ▲    │
│ Database changed                                        │
│ +----------+-----------+--------+                        │
│ | code     | name      | color  |                        │
│ +----------+-----------+--------+                        │
│ | 821/9735 | Harvest   | Beige  |                        │
│ | 821/9628 | Tempest   | Maroon |                        │
│ | 821/7355 | Dolphin   | Blue   |                        │
│ | 830/1921 | Daisy     | Lilac  |                        │
│ | 830/2078 | Starburst | White  |                        │
│ +----------+-----------+--------+                        │
│ 5 rows in set (0.00 sec)                                │
│                                                         │
│ Query OK, 1 row affected (0.00 sec)                     │
│                                                         │
│ Query OK, 1 row affected (0.00 sec)                     │
│                                                         │
│ +----------+-----------+--------+                        │
│ | code     | name      | color  |                        │
│ +----------+-----------+--------+                        │
│ | 821/9628 | Tempest   | Maroon |                        │
│ | 830/1921 | Daisy     | Lilac  |                        │
│ | 830/2078 | Starburst | White  |                        │
│ +----------+-----------+--------+                        │
│ 3 rows in set (0.00 sec)                                │
│                                                         │
│ Query OK, 3 rows affected (0.01 sec)                    │
│                                                         │
│ Empty set (0.00 sec)                                    │
│                                                         │
│ Query OK, 0 rows affected (0.00 sec)                    │
│                                                         │
│ Query OK, 0 rows affected (0.00 sec)                    │
│                                                         │
│ Empty set (0.00 sec)                                    │
│                                                         │
│ mysql> █                                           ▼    │
└────────────────────────────────────────────────────────┘
```

*If the WHERE part of a DELETE query is omitted the query will delete all rows – the data cannot be recovered.*

Notice that the DELETE queries in this example identify specific rows to delete by specifying their PRIMARY KEY "code" value after the WHERE keyword.

As with the previous UPDATE example, this is good practise – it prevents accidental deletion of data that can occur when other values are used to identify rows.

# Summary

- Data can be inserted into a database table with an INSERT INTO query

- The VALUES keyword is used in an INSERT INTO query to specify a list of data values as a comma-separated list within a single pair of parentheses

- All text data values must be surrounded by quotes

- The entire contents of a table can be revealed by a SELECT * FROM query

- It is advisable to include a columns list in every INSERT INTO query to explicitly identify columns where data is to be inserted

- Each INSERT INTO query inserts a single record into a table

- A single INSERT SELECT query can copy all the records in a table into another table

- All the fields in a column can be changed with an UPDATE query

- The WHERE keyword can be added to an UPDATE query to identify a specific row where a field is to be changed

- The SET keyword is used in an UPDATE query to change one, or more, fields in a row

- All the rows in a table can be deleted with a DELETE query

- The WHERE keyword can be added to a DELETE query to identify a specific row that is to be deleted

- Omitting the WHERE part of an UPDATE or DELETE query can accidentally change or delete all table data

- All tables should nominate a column to contain a PRIMARY KEY

- The WHERE keyword should always identify rows by their PRIMARY KEY value to prevent accidental changes to table data

# Retrieving data from tables

This chapter introduces the basic methods of retrieving data from within database tables. It demonstrates how to selectively retrieve specific columns and fields. Examples also illustrate how retrieved data can be dynamically stored in new tables.

## Covers

## Chapter Five

# Retrieving a column

The SQL query to view all data in a database table was introduced in the last chapter. The wildcard ★ character, meaning "all", can be replaced with a column name to retrieve only data from that particular column. The syntax of these SQL queries look like this:

```
SELECT * FROM table-name ;
SELECT column-name FROM table-name ;
```

The following SQL script first creates and populates a table. Then SELECT queries retrieve all its data and two specific columns.

*select-col.sql*
*(part of)*

```
# use the "my_database" database
USE my_database;

# create a table called "microwaves"
CREATE TABLE IF NOT EXISTS microwaves
(
  id       INT         AUTO_INCREMENT PRIMARY KEY,
  maker    VARCHAR(20) NOT NULL,
  model    VARCHAR(20) NOT NULL,
  power    INT         NOT NULL
);

# insert data into the "microwaves" table
INSERT INTO microwaves ( maker, model, power )
     VALUES ("Sharp", "R254SL", 800);
INSERT INTO microwaves ( maker, model, power )
     VALUES ("Sharp", "R33STM", 900);
INSERT INTO microwaves ( maker, model, power )
     VALUES ("Sanyo", "EMS3553", 900);
INSERT INTO microwaves ( maker, model, power )
     VALUES ("Panasonic", "NNE442", 900);
INSERT INTO microwaves ( maker, model, power )
     VALUES ("Daewoo", "KDR3000", 800);

# show all data in the "microwaves" database
SELECT * FROM microwaves;

# show all data in the "maker" column
SELECT maker FROM microwaves;
```

*select-col.sql*
*(cont'd)*

```
# show all data in the "model" column
SELECT model FROM microwaves;

# delete this sample table
DROP TABLE IF EXISTS microwaves;
```

*Some DBMS'
may return the
column values in
a different order
– but the result of
the query is still the same.*

```
MySQL Command Line Client                        _ □ ✕

mysql> source C:\SQL\select-col.sql
Database changed
Query OK, 0 rows affected (0.41 sec)

Query OK, 1 row affected (0.08 sec)

Query OK, 1 row affected (0.03 sec)

Query OK, 1 row affected (0.02 sec)

Query OK, 1 row affected (0.02 sec)

Query OK, 1 row affected (0.03 sec)

+----+-----------+---------+-------+
| id | maker     | model   | power |
+----+-----------+---------+-------+
|  1 | Sharp     | R254SL  |   800 |
|  2 | Sharp     | R33STM  |   900 |
|  3 | Sanyo     | EMS3553 |   900 |
|  4 | Panasonic | NNE442  |   900 |
|  5 | Daewoo    | KDR3000 |   800 |
+----+-----------+---------+-------+
5 rows in set (0.01 sec)

+-----------+
| maker     |
+-----------+
| Sharp     |
| Sharp     |
| Sanyo     |
| Panasonic |
| Daewoo    |
+-----------+
5 rows in set (0.00 sec)

+---------+
| model   |
+---------+
| R254SL  |
| R33STM  |
| EMS3553 |
| NNE442  |
| KDR3000 |
+---------+
5 rows in set (0.00 sec)

Query OK, 0 rows affected (0.14 sec)
```

# Retrieving multiple columns

A SELECT query can return the data from multiple columns by including the required column names as a comma-delimited list in the query. The syntax to get multiple column data looks like this:

```
SELECT column , column , column FROM table-name ;
```

This example builds the same table that was used in the previous example then retrieves two sets of multiple column data.

*select-cols.sql*
*(part of)*

```
USE my_database;    # use the "my_database" database

# create a table called "microwaves"
CREATE TABLE IF NOT EXISTS microwaves
(
  id        INT          AUTO_INCREMENT PRIMARY KEY,
  maker     VARCHAR(20)  NOT NULL,
  model     VARCHAR(20)  NOT NULL,
  power     INT          NOT NULL
);

# insert data into the "microwaves" table
INSERT INTO microwaves ( maker, model, power )
    VALUES ("Sharp", "R254SL", 800);
INSERT INTO microwaves ( maker, model, power )
    VALUES ("Sharp", "R33STM", 900);
INSERT INTO microwaves ( maker, model, power )
    VALUES ("Sanyo", "EMS3553", 900);
INSERT INTO microwaves ( maker, model, power )
    VALUES ("Panasonic", "NNE442", 900);
INSERT INTO microwaves ( maker, model, power )
    VALUES ("Daewoo", "KDR3000", 800);

# show all data in the "microwaves" database
SELECT * FROM microwaves;

# show all data in the "id" and "maker" columns
SELECT id, maker FROM microwaves;

# show all data in the "model" and "power" columns
SELECT model, power FROM microwaves;
```

*select-cols.sql*
*(cont'd)*

```
# delete this sample table
DROP TABLE IF EXISTS microwaves;
```

```
MySQL Command Line Client                                    _ □ ✕

mysql> source C:\SQL\select-cols.sql
Database changed
Query OK, 0 rows affected (0.08 sec)

Query OK, 1 row affected (0.04 sec)

Query OK, 1 row affected (0.01 sec)

Query OK, 1 row affected (0.03 sec)

Query OK, 1 row affected (0.02 sec)

Query OK, 1 row affected (0.03 sec)

+----+-----------+----------+-------+
| id | maker     | model    | power |
+----+-----------+----------+-------+
|  1 | Sharp     | R254SL   |   800 |
|  2 | Sharp     | R33STM   |   900 |
|  3 | Sanyo     | EMS3553  |   900 |
|  4 | Panasonic | NNE442   |   900 |
|  5 | Daewoo    | KDR3000  |   800 |
+----+-----------+----------+-------+
5 rows in set (0.00 sec)

+----+-----------+
| id | maker     |
+----+-----------+
|  1 | Sharp     |
|  2 | Sharp     |
|  3 | Sanyo     |
|  4 | Panasonic |
|  5 | Daewoo    |
+----+-----------+
5 rows in set (0.00 sec)

+----------+-------+
| model    | power |
+----------+-------+
| R254SL   |   800 |
| R33STM   |   900 |
| EMS3553  |   900 |
| NNE442   |   900 |
| KDR3000  |   800 |
+----------+-------+
5 rows in set (0.00 sec)

Query OK, 0 rows affected (0.02 sec)

mysql> _
```

# Retrieving a row

A SELECT query can retrieve a specific row from a database table if it includes the WHERE keyword to identify the required row. The row should be identified by its PRIMARY KEY value to prevent possible duplication. The syntax of a SELECT query to retrieve a specific row looks like this:

```
SELECT * FROM table-name WHERE column = value ;
```

The following SQL script once again builds the table from the previous examples. An initial SELECT query displays all the data within that table. Then two further SELECT queries display specific rows that are identified by their PRIMARY KEY values.

In this case the "microwaves" table is not deleted at the end of the SQL script so it can be used by examples later in this chapter.

*select-rows.sql*
*(part of)*

```
# use the "my_database" database
USE my_database;

# create a table called "microwaves"
CREATE TABLE IF NOT EXISTS microwaves
(
  id       INT          AUTO_INCREMENT PRIMARY KEY,
  maker    VARCHAR(20)  NOT NULL,
  model    VARCHAR(20)  NOT NULL,
  power    INT          NOT NULL
);

# insert data into the "microwaves" table
INSERT INTO microwaves ( maker, model, power )
    VALUES ("Sharp", "R254SL", 800);
INSERT INTO microwaves ( maker, model, power )
    VALUES ("Sharp", "R33STM", 900);
INSERT INTO microwaves ( maker, model, power )
    VALUES ("Sanyo", "EMS3553", 900);
INSERT INTO microwaves ( maker, model, power )
    VALUES ("Panasonic", "NNE442", 900);
INSERT INTO microwaves ( maker, model, power )
    VALUES ("Daewoo", "KDR3000", 800);
```

*select-rows.sql*
*(cont'd)*

```
# show all data in the "microwaves" database
SELECT * FROM microwaves;

# show all data in row 2
SELECT * FROM microwaves WHERE id = 2;

# show all data in row 4
SELECT * FROM microwaves WHERE id = 4;
```

```
MySQL Command Line Client                              _ □ ×

mysql> source C:\SQL\select-rows.sql
Database changed
Query OK, 0 rows affected (0.08 sec)

Query OK, 1 row affected (0.02 sec)

Query OK, 1 row affected (0.02 sec)

Query OK, 1 row affected (0.02 sec)

Query OK, 1 row affected (0.03 sec)

Query OK, 1 row affected (0.02 sec)

+----+-----------+----------+-------+
| id | maker     | model    | power |
+----+-----------+----------+-------+
|  1 | Sharp     | R254SL   |   800 |
|  2 | Sharp     | R33STM   |   900 |
|  3 | Sanyo     | EMS3553  |   900 |
|  4 | Panasonic | NNE442   |   900 |
|  5 | Daewoo    | KDR3000  |   800 |
+----+-----------+----------+-------+
5 rows in set (0.00 sec)

+----+--------+--------+-------+
| id | maker  | model  | power |
+----+--------+--------+-------+
|  2 | Sharp  | R33STM |   900 |
+----+--------+--------+-------+
1 row in set (0.12 sec)

+----+-----------+--------+-------+
| id | maker     | model  | power |
+----+-----------+--------+-------+
|  4 | Panasonic | NNE442 |   900 |
+----+-----------+--------+-------+
1 row in set (0.02 sec)

mysql> _
```

*SQL queries comprise one, or more "clauses". Each clause consists of a keyword and data. For instance, WHERE id = 3 is known as a WHERE clause.*

# Copying retrieved data

Database tables can be created dynamically by combining a CREATE TABLE query with a SELECT query. The SELECT query can copy all rows, or specific rows, into the new table to populate its columns. The new table inherits the column names and features from the table from which the data is being copied.

This example dynamically creates two new tables by copying specific rows from the "microwaves" table created in the previous example. It uses the values in its "power" column to select specific rows to populate each of the new tables.

*copy-rows.sql*

```
# use the "my_database" database
USE my_database;

# create a table called "800w_microwaves" and
# copy all 800w microwave data from "microwaves"
CREATE TABLE IF NOT EXISTS 800w_microwaves
SELECT * FROM microwaves WHERE power = 800;

# create a table called "900w_microwaves" and
# copy all 900w microwave data from "microwaves"
CREATE TABLE IF NOT EXISTS 900w_microwaves
SELECT * FROM microwaves WHERE power = 900;

# show all existing tables
SHOW TABLES;

# show all data in the "microwaves" database
SELECT * FROM microwaves;

# show all data in the "800w_microwaves" database
SELECT * FROM 800w_microwaves;

# show all data in the "900w_microwaves" database
SELECT * FROM 900w_microwaves;

# delete sample tables
DROP TABLE IF EXISTS 800w_microwaves;
DROP TABLE IF EXISTS 900w_microwaves;

# show all existing tables
SHOW TABLES;
```

```
MySQL Command Line Client                                    _ □ ✕

Database changed
Query OK, 2 rows affected (0.15 sec)
Records: 2  Duplicates: 0  Warnings: 0

Query OK, 3 rows affected (0.10 sec)
Records: 3  Duplicates: 0  Warnings: 0

+------------------------+
| Tables_in_my_database  |
+------------------------+
| 800w_microwaves        |
| 900w_microwaves        |
| microwaves             |
+------------------------+
3 rows in set (0.05 sec)

+-----+-----------+----------+---------+
| id  | maker     | model    | power   |
+-----+-----------+----------+---------+
|  1  | Sharp     | R254SL   |    800  |
|  2  | Sharp     | R33STM   |    900  |
|  3  | Sanyo     | EMS3553  |    900  |
|  4  | Panasonic | NNE442   |    900  |
|  5  | Daewoo    | KDR3000  |    800  |
+-----+-----------+----------+---------+
5 rows in set (0.00 sec)

+-----+-----------+----------+---------+
| id  | maker     | model    | power   |
+-----+-----------+----------+---------+
|  1  | Sharp     | R254SL   |    800  |
|  5  | Daewoo    | KDR3000  |    800  |
+-----+-----------+----------+---------+
2 rows in set (0.01 sec)

+-----+-----------+----------+---------+
| id  | maker     | model    | power   |
+-----+-----------+----------+---------+
|  2  | Sharp     | R33STM   |    900  |
|  3  | Sanyo     | EMS3553  |    900  |
|  4  | Panasonic | NNE442   |    900  |
+-----+-----------+----------+---------+
3 rows in set (0.00 sec)

Query OK, 0 rows affected (0.04 sec)

Query OK, 0 rows affected (0.01 sec)

+------------------------+
| Tables_in_my_database  |
+------------------------+
| microwaves             |
+------------------------+
1 row in set (0.01 sec)

mysql> _
```

*Add EXPLAIN queries to this script to confirm that each new table inherits the column values from the original table.*

# Inserting multiple selected fields

Specific fields of a table can be copied into specific fields of another table using an INSERT INTO query. This must state a row identifier and the column names of both the source column and the destination column. Its syntax looks like this:

```
INSERT INTO table-name ( column , column )
SELECT column , column WHERE column = value ;
```

The following SQL script first creates a table called "sharp-ovens" with two rows of data. An INSERT INTO query then copies two specific fields from the "microwaves" table, used in previous examples, into specific fields of the "sharp_ovens" table.

copy-fields.sql
(part of)

```
USE my_database;    # use the "my_database" database

# create a table called "sharp_ovens"
CREATE TABLE sharp_ovens
(
    id        INT           AUTO_INCREMENT PRIMARY KEY,
    model     VARCHAR(20)   NOT NULL,
    power     INT           NOT NULL,
    grill     VARCHAR(3)    DEFAULT "No"
);

# insert data into the "sharp_ovens" table
INSERT INTO sharp_ovens (model, power, grill)
     VALUES ("R654", 800, "Yes");
INSERT INTO sharp_ovens (model, power, grill)
     VALUES ("R64ST", 800, "Yes");

# show all data in the "microwaves" table
SELECT * FROM microwaves;

# show all data in the "sharp_ovens" table
SELECT * FROM sharp_ovens;

# copy specific fields from "microwaves" to "sharp_ovens"
INSERT INTO sharp_ovens (model, power)
SELECT model, power FROM microwaves
WHERE maker = "Sharp";
```

copy-fields.sql
(cont'd)

```
# show all data in the "sharp_ovens" table
SELECT * FROM sharp_ovens;

# delete sample tables used in this chapter
DROP TABLE microwaves;
DROP TABLE sharp_ovens;
```

```
MySQL Command Line Client                                  _ □ ×

mysql> source C:\SQL\copy-fields.sql
Database changed
Query OK, 0 rows affected (0.07 sec)

Query OK, 1 row affected (0.02 sec)

Query OK, 1 row affected (0.04 sec)

+----+-----------+----------+--------+
| id | maker     | model    | power  |
+----+-----------+----------+--------+
|  1 | Sharp     | R254SL   |    800 |
|  2 | Sharp     | R33STM   |    900 |
|  3 | Sanyo     | EMS3553  |    900 |
|  4 | Panasonic | NNE442   |    900 |
|  5 | Daewoo    | KDR3000  |    800 |
+----+-----------+----------+--------+
5 rows in set (0.01 sec)

+----+--------+--------+--------+
| id | model  | power  | grill  |
+----+--------+--------+--------+
|  1 | R654   |    800 | Yes    |
|  2 | R64ST  |    800 | Yes    |
+----+--------+--------+--------+
2 rows in set (0.00 sec)

Query OK, 2 rows affected (0.05 sec)
Records: 2  Duplicates: 0  Warnings: 0

+----+--------+--------+--------+
| id | model  | power  | grill  |
+----+--------+--------+--------+
|  1 | R654   |    800 | Yes    |
|  2 | R64ST  |    800 | Yes    |
|  3 | R254SL |    800 | No     |
|  4 | R33STM |    900 | No     |
+----+--------+--------+--------+
4 rows in set (0.00 sec)

Query OK, 0 rows affected (0.04 sec)

Query OK, 0 rows affected (0.03 sec)

mysql> _
```

# Summary

- The entire contents of a table can be revealed by a SELECT * FROM query

- A SELECT query can reveal the contents of a specific column by stating the column name in place of the * wildcard character

- Multiple column data can be retrieved by stating the column names as a comma-delimited list in a SELECT query

- A specific row can be retrieved from a table by adding the WHERE keyword to a SELECT query to identify the row

- The CREATE TABLE query can be combined with a SELECT query to dynamically create a new table populated with data from the selected existing table

- SQL queries comprise a number of statements which are known as "clauses"

- A WHERE clause can be added to a combined CREATE TABLE and SELECT query to retrieve data from specific rows

- An INSERT INTO query can be combined with a SELECT query to copy data from specific fields of one table into specific fields of another table

- A WHERE clause can be added to a combined INSERT INTO and SELECT query to retrieve data from specific rows

# Sorting retrieved data

This chapter illustrates how retrieved data can be sorted in a variety of ways. Examples demonstrate how to sort data alphabetically or numerically in ascending or descending order.

## Covers

Chapter Six

# Sorting a column

The data returned by a SELECT query may not always appear in the same order as the rows of the table – especially following updates to that table. The retrieved data can, however, be explicitly sorted into a specified order using an ORDER BY clause.

When the ORDER BY keywords are followed by a table column name, the retrieved data will be sorted into order based upon the type of data in the specified column. Typically, if the column data type is numerical the retrieved data will be sorted in ascending numerical order. If the column data type is textual the retrieved data will be sorted into alphabetical order from A through Z.

The SQL example script listed below demonstrates both numerical and alphabetical sorting of retrieved data.

*sort-data.sql*

```
# use the "my_database" database
USE my_database;

# create a table called "critters"
CREATE TABLE critters
(
  id        INT         PRIMARY KEY,
  name      VARCHAR(20) NOT NULL
);

# insert 5 records into the "critters" table
INSERT INTO critters (id, name) VALUES (3,"Beaver");
INSERT INTO critters (id, name) VALUES (1,"Duck");
INSERT INTO critters (id, name) VALUES (4,"Aardvark");
INSERT INTO critters (id, name) VALUES (2,"Elephant");
INSERT INTO critters (id, name) VALUES (5,"Camel");

# show all data in the "critters" table
SELECT * FROM critters;

# show all data in "critters" numerically ordered
SELECT * FROM critters ORDER BY id;

# show the "name" column in "critters" alphabetically
SELECT name FROM critters ORDER BY name;

# delete this sample table
DROP TABLE critters;
```

*An ORDER BY clause must only appear as the final clause of a SELECT query – otherwise an error is generated.*

*Data retrieved from a column can be sorted by the order of another column whose data is not actually retrieved.*

```
Linux - Shell - Konsole

Session  Edit  View  Bookmarks  Settings  Help

mysql> source /home/SQL/sort-data.sql
Database changed
Query OK, 0 rows affected (0.01 sec)

Query OK, 1 row affected (0.00 sec)

Query OK, 1 row affected (0.00 sec)

Query OK, 1 row affected (0.00 sec)

Query OK, 1 row affected (0.00 sec)

Query OK, 1 row affected (0.00 sec)

+----+----------+
| id | name     |
+----+----------+
|  3 | Beaver   |
|  1 | Duck     |
|  4 | Aardvark |
|  2 | Elephant |
|  5 | Camel    |
+----+----------+
5 rows in set (0.01 sec)

+----+----------+
| id | name     |
+----+----------+
|  1 | Duck     |
|  2 | Elephant |
|  3 | Beaver   |
|  4 | Aardvark |
|  5 | Camel    |
+----+----------+
5 rows in set (0.00 sec)

+----------+
| name     |
+----------+
| Aardvark |
| Beaver   |
| Camel    |
| Duck     |
| Elephant |
+----------+
5 rows in set (0.00 sec)

Query OK, 0 rows affected (0.00 sec)
```

# Sorting multiple columns

An ORDER BY clause can sort retrieved data by multiple columns and the SQL script below demonstrates how this can be useful. This example sorts a number of name values into alphabetical order – firstly by last name, then by first name. Note that sorting by first name, then by last name does not produce the same result.

*sort-multi.sql*

```
# use the "my_database" database
USE my_database;

# create a table called "employees"
CREATE TABLE employees
(
  id         INT         AUTO_INCREMENT PRIMARY KEY,
  first_name VARCHAR(20) NOT NULL,
  last_name  VARCHAR(20) NOT NULL
);

# insert 7 records into the "employees" table
INSERT INTO employees (first_name, last_name)
    VALUES ("Arthur", "Smith");
INSERT INTO employees (first_name, last_name)
    VALUES ("Peter", "Jones");
INSERT INTO employees (first_name, last_name)
    VALUES ("Ann", "Smith");
INSERT INTO employees (first_name, last_name)
    VALUES ("Sandra", "Williams");
INSERT INTO employees (first_name, last_name)
    VALUES ("Andrew", "Smith");
INSERT INTO employees (first_name, last_name)
    VALUES ("Paul", "Jones");
INSERT INTO employees (first_name, last_name)
    VALUES ("Sally", "Williams");

# show all data in the "employees" table
SELECT * FROM employees;

# show both names sorted alphabetically
SELECT first_name, last_name FROM employees
ORDER BY last_name, first_name;

# delete this sample table
DROP TABLE employees;
```

```
Linux - Shell - Konsole

Session Edit View Bookmarks Settings Help

mysql> source /home/SQL/sort-multi.sql
Database changed
Query OK, 0 rows affected (0.01 sec)

Query OK, 1 row affected (0.01 sec)

Query OK, 1 row affected (0.00 sec)

Query OK, 1 row affected (0.00 sec)

Query OK, 1 row affected (0.00 sec)

Query OK, 1 row affected (0.00 sec)

Query OK, 1 row affected (0.00 sec)

Query OK, 1 row affected (0.00 sec)

+----+------------+----------+
| id | first_name | last_name |
+----+------------+----------+
|  1 | Arthur     | Smith    |
|  2 | Peter      | Jones    |
|  3 | Ann        | Smith    |
|  4 | Sandra     | Williams |
|  5 | Andrew     | Smith    |
|  6 | Paul       | Jones    |
|  7 | Sally      | Williams |
+----+------------+----------+
7 rows in set (0.00 sec)

+------------+----------+
| first_name | last_name |
+------------+----------+
| Paul       | Jones    |
| Peter      | Jones    |
| Andrew     | Smith    |
| Ann        | Smith    |
| Arthur     | Smith    |
| Sally      | Williams |
| Sandra     | Williams |
+------------+----------+
7 rows in set (0.01 sec)

Query OK, 0 rows affected (0.00 sec)

mysql> █
```

*Amend this script to ORDER BY first_name, last_name then compare the result to that shown in this screenshot.*

# Sorting by column position

The ORDER BY clause can optionally refer to a column of retrieved data by its position rather than its name. For instance, the first column is position 1, the next is position 2, and so on. Care must be taken to recognize that the position is that of <u>retrieved</u> columns only – not of all the columns in the table.

In the example below, the SELECT query returns three columns. The ORDER BY clause refers to the retrieved "price" column at position 3 – even though it is at position 4 in the original table.

*sort-bypos.sql*

```
USE my_database;    # use the "my_database" database

# create a table called "watches"
CREATE TABLE watches
(
  id        INT         AUTO_INCREMENT PRIMARY KEY,
  model     VARCHAR(20)  NOT NULL,
  style     VARCHAR(6)   DEFAULT "Gents",
  price     DECIMAL(3,2) NOT NULL
);

# insert 5 records into the "watches" table
INSERT INTO watches (model, price)
    VALUES ("Panama", 69.99);
INSERT INTO watches (model, style, price)
    VALUES ("Club", "Ladies", 59.99);
INSERT INTO watches (model, price)
    VALUES ("Avante", 49.99);
INSERT INTO watches (model, style, price)
    VALUES ("Panama", "Ladies", 69.99);
INSERT INTO watches (model, price)
    VALUES ("Club", 59.99);

# show all data in the "watches" table
SELECT * FROM watches;

# show data in "watches" ordered by style
SELECT model, style, price FROM watches ORDER BY 2;

# show data in "watches" in ascending price order
SELECT model, style, price FROM watches ORDER BY 3;

DROP TABLE watches;        # delete this sample table
```

*This technique cannot be used when sorting by a column that is not retrieved – the ORDER BY clause must use the column name in that case.*

*If the columns specified in the SELECT list get changed, the ORDER BY positions may need to be changed accordingly.*

```
Linux - Shell - Konsole
Session  Edit  View  Bookmarks  Settings  Help

mysql> source /home/SQL/sort-bypos.sql
Database changed
Query OK, 0 rows affected (0.01 sec)

Query OK, 1 row affected (0.00 sec)

Query OK, 1 row affected (0.00 sec)

Query OK, 1 row affected (0.00 sec)

Query OK, 1 row affected (0.00 sec)

Query OK, 1 row affected (0.01 sec)

+----+--------+--------+-------+
| id | model  | style  | price |
+----+--------+--------+-------+
|  1 | Panama | Gents  | 69.99 |
|  2 | Club   | Ladies | 59.99 |
|  3 | Avante | Gents  | 49.99 |
|  4 | Panama | Ladies | 69.99 |
|  5 | Club   | Gents  | 59.99 |
+----+--------+--------+-------+
5 rows in set (0.00 sec)

+--------+--------+-------+
| model  | style  | price |
+--------+--------+-------+
| Panama | Gents  | 69.99 |
| Avante | Gents  | 49.99 |
| Club   | Gents  | 59.99 |
| Club   | Ladies | 59.99 |
| Panama | Ladies | 69.99 |
+--------+--------+-------+
5 rows in set (0.00 sec)

+--------+--------+-------+
| model  | style  | price |
+--------+--------+-------+
| Avante | Gents  | 49.99 |
| Club   | Ladies | 59.99 |
| Club   | Gents  | 59.99 |
| Panama | Gents  | 69.99 |
| Panama | Ladies | 69.99 |
+--------+--------+-------+
5 rows in set (0.00 sec)

Query OK, 0 rows affected (0.00 sec)
```

*Although this technique means the column names need not be typed, it is easier to mistake columns – use column names rather than retrieved column positions to avoid confusion.*

# Setting the sort direction

By default SELECT queries are automatically sorted in ascending order. An ORDER BY clause can explicitly specify the sort direction by adding the keywords DESC (descending) or ASC (ascending) after the name of the column to sort by.

In the SQL script listed below, the ASC and DESC keywords are used to determine the sort direction for three columns of data.

*sort-dir.sql*

```
# use the "my_database" database
USE my_database;

# create a table called "top_5_films"
CREATE TABLE top_5_films
(
   position   INT          PRIMARY KEY,
   title      VARCHAR(25)  NOT NULL,
   year       INT          NOT NULL
);

# insert 5 records into the "top_5" table
INSERT INTO top_5_films (position, title, year)
     VALUES (1, "Citizen Kane", 1941);
INSERT INTO top_5_films (position, title, year)
     VALUES (2, "Casablanca",1942);
INSERT INTO top_5_films (position, title, year)
     VALUES (3, "The Godfather", 1972);
INSERT INTO top_5_films (position, title, year)
     VALUES (4, "Gone With The Wind", 1939);
INSERT INTO top_5_films (position, title, year)
     VALUES (5, "Lawrence Of Arabia", 1962);

# show all data in "top_5_films" by descending position
SELECT * FROM top_5_films ORDER BY position DESC;

# show all data in "top_5_films" by ascending year
SELECT * FROM top_5_films ORDER BY year ASC;

# show all data in "top_5_films" in alphabetical order
SELECT * FROM top_5_films ORDER BY title ASC;

# delete this sample table
DROP TABLE top_5_films;
```

*Opinions may be divided on the top five films of all time – the data in this example represents the choice of the American Film Institute.*

Add the DESC keyword after each column name in the ORDER BY clause when sorting on multiple columns.

```
Linux - Shell - Konsole

Session  Edit  View  Bookmarks  Settings  Help

mysql> source /home/SQL/sort-dir.sql
Database changed
Query OK, 0 rows affected (0.01 sec)

Query OK, 1 row affected (0.00 sec)

Query OK, 1 row affected (0.00 sec)

Query OK, 1 row affected (0.00 sec)

Query OK, 1 row affected (0.00 sec)

Query OK, 1 row affected (0.01 sec)

+----------+---------------------+------+
| position | title               | year |
+----------+---------------------+------+
|        5 | Lawrence Of Arabia  | 1962 |
|        4 | Gone With The Wind  | 1939 |
|        3 | The Godfather       | 1972 |
|        2 | Casablanca          | 1942 |
|        1 | Citizen Kane        | 1941 |
+----------+---------------------+------+
5 rows in set (0.00 sec)

+----------+---------------------+------+
| position | title               | year |
+----------+---------------------+------+
|        4 | Gone With The Wind  | 1939 |
|        1 | Citizen Kane        | 1941 |
|        2 | Casablanca          | 1942 |
|        5 | Lawrence Of Arabia  | 1962 |
|        3 | The Godfather       | 1972 |
+----------+---------------------+------+
5 rows in set (0.00 sec)

+----------+---------------------+------+
| position | title               | year |
+----------+---------------------+------+
|        2 | Casablanca          | 1942 |
|        1 | Citizen Kane        | 1941 |
|        4 | Gone With The Wind  | 1939 |
|        5 | Lawrence Of Arabia  | 1962 |
|        3 | The Godfather       | 1972 |
+----------+---------------------+------+
5 rows in set (0.00 sec)

Query OK, 0 rows affected (0.00 sec)
```

The default behavior when sorting treats "a" the same as "A" – but these can be treated as different values if the DBMS configuration has been modified to do so.

# Summary

- The data returned by a SELECT query may not appear in the same order as it does in the database table

- An ORDER BY clause can be added to a SELECT query to explicitly specify how the retrieved data should be ordered

- The ORDER BY keywords specify a column upon which to order the retrieved data

- If the column specified to sort by contains a textual data type the retrieved data will, by default, be sorted alphabetically A – Z

- If the column specified to sort by contains numerical data the retrieved data will, by default, be sorted numerically in ascending order. For instance, 1 – 1000

- An ORDER BY clause can only appear as the final clause in a SELECT query

- An ORDER BY clause can specify multiple columns to sort by. This is particularly useful to sort names into alphabetical order by both first name and last name

- The column to sort by in an ORDER BY clause can alternatively be referred to by its ordinal position in the retrieved data

- When referencing the column to sort by using its position, any changes to columns in the SELECT list may need to be reflected in changes to the ORDER BY clause

- The sort direction can be explicitly specified by adding either ASC or DESC in the ORDER BY clause

# Simple data filtering

This chapter demonstrates how SELECT queries can retrieve specific data by stating a comparative test. It introduces the various comparison operators that can be used to make selective comparisons. Examples illustrate how data can be retrieved from a database table following a comparative test.

## Covers

Chapter Seven

# Making comparisons

The database tables in the examples in this book only contain a few records because of space limitations – in reality, database tables usually contain many records.

Queries against large database tables generally seek a subset of the table's data rather than its entire contents. This is achieved by stating a "search criteria" in the SQL query.

In a **SELECT** query the search criteria can be specified in its **WHERE** clause, using a comparison operator to test whether a condition is met in any particular record. When the condition is met the query will return the data in that record – when the test fails no data will be returned.

Each comparison is an evaluation that is "true" when the test succeeds and "false" when the test fails.

The equality comparison operator, represented by the = character, was introduced in the example on page 66. This compares a database table's field value with a specified test value, then returns data from that record only when the comparison is true. When the comparison is false no data is returned by the query.

Making comparative tests in this way allows the data returned by an SQL query to be selectively filtered according to the requirements of the query.

It is, of course, also possible to make an SQL query to retrieve all the data in a table from an application that subsequently filters the data according to requirements. For instance, a C++ client application could query a database to return all its records then loop through each record selecting specific data according to given search criteria.

This is, however, a slower and less efficient technique – all DBMS software is optimized to provide fast and accurate filtration of data stored within database tables. It is recommended that it should always be the SQL query that filters the data rather than the application making the query.

In addition to the equality operator, introduced earlier, there are a number of other comparison operators that can be used in a WHERE clause to specify search criteria.

The comparison operators vary from one DBMS to another but the most commonly recognized comparison operators are listed in the table below:

*Check the documentation for your DBMS to discover if these and other comparison operators are supported.*

| Operator | Description |
| --- | --- |
| = | Equality |
| != | Inequality |
| < | Less than |
| <= | Less than or equal |
| > | More than |
| >= | More than or equal |
| BETWEEN *min* AND *max* | Within the range *min* to *max* |
| IS NULL | Is a NULL value |
| IS NOT NULL | Is not a NULL value |

A frequently found alternative to the != inequality operator is the <> inequality operator. This book uses the != version because that also appears in other languages, such as JavaScript.

Examples that follow in the rest of this chapter demonstrate how each of the comparison operators can be used to select specific data from a database table.

# Comparing a single value

The most simple comparison in a SELECT query's WHERE clause just compares a specified field on each row against a given value. When the comparison is true the data is retrieved from that row – otherwise that row is ignored.

The following SQL script demonstrates the comparison of the value contained in each row of a table column named "price" against a specified value. In this case all the data from a row where the comparison is true is retrieved by the SELECT query. The data returned by the queries in this example illustrates the difference between the < "less than" operator, > "greater than" operator and the <= "less than or equal to" operator.

*filter-one.sql*
*(part of)*

```
# use the "my_database" database
USE my_database;

# create a table called "clock radios"
CREATE TABLE IF NOT EXISTS clock_radios
(
    code        CHAR(8)         PRIMARY KEY,
    make        VARCHAR(25)     NOT NULL,
    model       VARCHAR(25)     NOT NULL,
    price       DECIMAL(3,2)    NOT NULL
);

# insert 5 records into the "clock_radios" table
INSERT INTO clock_radios (code, make, model, price)
    VALUES ("512/4792", "Alba", "C2108", 6.75);
INSERT INTO clock_radios (code, make, model, price)
    VALUES ("512/4125", "Hitachi", "KC30", 8.99);
INSERT INTO clock_radios (code, make, model, price)
    VALUES ("512/1458", "Philips", "AJ3010", 19.99);
INSERT INTO clock_radios (code, make, model, price)
    VALUES ("512/3669","Morphy Richards","28025",19.99);
INSERT INTO clock_radios (code, make, model, price)
    VALUES ("512/1444", "Sony", "C253", 29.49);

# show records in "clock_radios" if price is below 19.99
SELECT * FROM clock_radios WHERE price < 19.99;

# show records in "clock_radios" if price is above 19.99
SELECT * FROM clock_radios WHERE price > 19.99;
```

*filter-one.sql*
*(cont'd)*

```
# show records if price is either 19.99 or less
SELECT * FROM clock_radios WHERE price <= 19.99;

# delete this sample table
DROP TABLE IF EXISTS clock_radios;
```

*Values that are text "strings" must be surrounded by quotes.*

```
MySQL Command Line Client                    _ □ ×

mysql> source C:\SQL\filter-one.sql
Database changed
Query OK, 0 rows affected (0.44 sec)

Query OK, 1 row affected (0.06 sec)

Query OK, 1 row affected (0.02 sec)

Query OK, 1 row affected (0.02 sec)

Query OK, 1 row affected (0.02 sec)

Query OK, 1 row affected (0.02 sec)

+----------+---------+---------+---------+
| code     | make    | model   | price   |
+----------+---------+---------+---------+
| 512/4125 | Hitachi | KC30    |   8.99  |
| 512/4792 | Alba    | C2108   |   6.75  |
+----------+---------+---------+---------+
2 rows in set (0.06 sec)

+----------+---------+---------+---------+
| code     | make    | model   | price   |
+----------+---------+---------+---------+
| 512/1444 | Sony    | C253    |  29.49  |
+----------+---------+---------+---------+
1 row in set (0.02 sec)

+----------+-----------------+---------+---------+
| code     | make            | model   | price   |
+----------+-----------------+---------+---------+
| 512/1458 | Philips         | AJ3010  |  19.99  |
| 512/3669 | Morphy Richards | 28025   |  19.99  |
| 512/4125 | Hitachi         | KC30    |   8.99  |
| 512/4792 | Alba            | C2108   |   6.75  |
+----------+-----------------+---------+---------+
4 rows in set (0.00 sec)

Query OK, 0 rows affected (0.13 sec)

mysql> _
```

# Comparing a range of values

The **WHERE** clause in a **SELECT** query can test if the value in a column field falls within a specified range using the SQL keywords **BETWEEN** and **AND**. The syntax for such a query looks like this:

```
SELECT data FROM table-name
WHERE column BETWEEN min AND max ;
```

*Refer to the documentation for your own DBMS to see how it treats the BETWEEN and AND keywords.*

Minimum and maximum values can be specified numerically or alphabetically. The results returned by a **SELECT** query that specifies a range comparison can vary from one database to another. Some DBMS' return the data that is on the row that matches the specified minimum value in addition to that on other rows up to the specified maximum value. Other DBMS' only return the data for rows that truly match between the specified minimum and maximum values.

The SQL script listed below makes a **SELECT** query that retrieves data from those rows where the value in its "price" column falls within a specified numerical range. A second **SELECT** query retrieves data from those rows where the value in its "make" column falls within a specified alphabetical range.

*filter-range.sql
(part of)*

```
# use the "my_database" database
USE my_database;

# create a table called "treadmills"
CREATE TABLE IF NOT EXISTS treadmills
(
    code        CHAR(8)        PRIMARY KEY,
    make        VARCHAR(25)    NOT NULL,
    model       VARCHAR(25)    NOT NULL,
    price       INT            NOT NULL
);

# insert 5 records into the "treadmills" table
INSERT INTO treadmills (code, make, model, price)
    VALUES ("335/1914", "York", "Pacer 2120", 159);
INSERT INTO treadmills (code, make, model, price)
    VALUES ("335/1907", "York", "Pacer 2750", 349);
```

*filter-range.sql*
*(cont'd)*

```sql
INSERT INTO treadmills (code, make, model, price)
  VALUES ("335/1921", "York", "Pacer 3100", 499);
INSERT INTO treadmills (code, make, model, price)
  VALUES ("335/2717", "Proform", "7.25Q", 799);
INSERT INTO treadmills (code, make, model, price)
  VALUES ("335/2652", "Reebok", "TR1 Power Run", 895);

# show all records where the price is between 300 - 500
SELECT * FROM treadmills
  WHERE price BETWEEN 300 AND 500;

# show records where make is between "Proform" and "York"
SELECT * FROM treadmills
  WHERE make BETWEEN "P" AND "Y";

# delete this sample table
DROP TABLE IF EXISTS treadmills;
```

```
MySQL Command Line Client                              _ □ ✕

mysql> source C:\SQL\filter-range.sql
Database changed
Query OK, 0 rows affected (0.06 sec)

Query OK, 1 row affected (0.04 sec)

Query OK, 1 row affected (0.02 sec)

Query OK, 1 row affected (0.02 sec)

Query OK, 1 row affected (0.03 sec)

Query OK, 1 row affected (0.02 sec)

+----------+------+------------+-------+
| code     | make | model      | price |
+----------+------+------------+-------+
| 335/1907 | York | Pacer 2750 |   349 |
| 335/1921 | York | Pacer 3100 |   499 |
+----------+------+------------+-------+
2 rows in set (0.02 sec)

+----------+---------+---------------+-------+
| code     | make    | model         | price |
+----------+---------+---------------+-------+
| 335/2652 | Reebok  | TR1 Power Run |   895 |
| 335/2717 | Proform | 7.25Q         |   799 |
+----------+---------+---------------+-------+
2 rows in set (0.01 sec)

Query OK, 0 rows affected (0.03 sec)
```

*MySQL includes the data from the row matching the specified minimum value "Proform" in this example – other DBMS' may not.*

# Seeking non-matches

The != inequality operator can be used in the WHERE clause of a SELECT query to retrieve data from table rows that do not match a specified value in the tested column.

The following SQL script demonstrates how only non-matching rows can be retrieved. It first creates a table then displays its entire contents. A SELECT query first uses the = equality operator to display records that do match a specified value. Conversely, a final SELECT query uses the != inequality operator to display the other records that do not match the specified value.

*filter-notequal.sql*
*(part of)*

```
# use the "my_database" database
USE my_database;

# create a table called "office_chairs"
CREATE TABLE IF NOT EXISTS office_chairs
(
    code      CHAR(8)       PRIMARY KEY,
    model     VARCHAR(25)   NOT NULL,
    fabric    VARCHAR(25)   DEFAULT "Cloth",
    price     DECIMAL(6,2)  NOT NULL
);

# insert 5 records into the "office_chairs" table
INSERT INTO office_chairs (code, model, price)
    VALUES ("617/9148", "Clerk", 19.99);
INSERT INTO office_chairs (code, model, price)
    VALUES ("617/8156", "Secretary", 34.99);
INSERT INTO office_chairs (code, model, fabric, price)
    VALUES ("617/9131", "Manager", "Leather", 49.99);
INSERT INTO office_chairs (code, model, fabric, price)
    VALUES ("621/0258", "Captain", "Wood", 99.99);
INSERT INTO office_chairs (code, model, fabric, price)
    VALUES ("619/6444", "Executive", "Leather", 124.99);

# show all data in the "office_chairs" table
SELECT * FROM office_chairs;

# show all records where the fabric is "Leather"
SELECT * FROM office_chairs WHERE fabric = "Leather";
```

*filter-notequal.sql*
*(cont'd)*

```
# show all records where the fabric is not "Leather"
SELECT * FROM office_chairs WHERE fabric != "Leather";

# delete this sample table
DROP TABLE IF EXISTS office_chairs;
```

*Unlike some other DBMS' MySQL does not support !< "not less than" or !> "not greater than" syntax – these are simply the same as > "greater than" and < "less than" respectively.*

```
MySQL Command Line Client

mysql> source C:\SQL\filter-notequal.sql
Database changed
Query OK, 0 rows affected (0.07 sec)

Query OK, 1 row affected (0.02 sec)

Query OK, 1 row affected (0.02 sec)

Query OK, 1 row affected (0.02 sec)

Query OK, 1 row affected (0.03 sec)

Query OK, 1 row affected (0.02 sec)

+----------+-----------+---------+--------+
| code     | model     | fabric  | price  |
+----------+-----------+---------+--------+
| 617/8156 | Secretary | Cloth   |  34.99 |
| 617/9131 | Manager   | Leather |  49.99 |
| 617/9148 | Clerk     | Cloth   |  19.99 |
| 619/6444 | Executive | Leather | 124.99 |
| 621/0258 | Captain   | Wood    |  99.99 |
+----------+-----------+---------+--------+
5 rows in set (0.00 sec)

+----------+-----------+---------+--------+
| code     | model     | fabric  | price  |
+----------+-----------+---------+--------+
| 617/9131 | Manager   | Leather |  49.99 |
| 619/6444 | Executive | Leather | 124.99 |
+----------+-----------+---------+--------+
2 rows in set (0.00 sec)

+----------+-----------+--------+-------+
| code     | model     | fabric | price |
+----------+-----------+--------+-------+
| 617/8156 | Secretary | Cloth  | 34.99 |
| 617/9148 | Clerk     | Cloth  | 19.99 |
| 621/0258 | Captain   | Wood   | 99.99 |
+----------+-----------+--------+-------+
3 rows in set (0.00 sec)

Query OK, 0 rows affected (0.03 sec)

mysql> _
```

# Finding null values

The SQL keywords **IS NULL** can be used in the **WHERE** clause of a **SELECT** query to retrieve data from table records that have no value in the tested column field. Recall that the column definition must permit that column to contain empty fields.

The "color" column in the SQL example below allows a color to be optionally stored – if no color is specified, that field will contain a **NULL** value by default. An **EXPLAIN** query confirms the table format then all that table's data is displayed. A **SELECT** query then retrieves the data from rows where no color value is stated.

*filter-null.sql*
*(part of)*

*A NULL value represents a completely empty field – it is not the same as zero or an "" empty string.*

```
# use the "my_database" database
USE my_database;

# create a table called "steam_irons"
CREATE TABLE IF NOT EXISTS steam_irons
(
    id      INT          AUTO_INCREMENT PRIMARY KEY,
    make    VARCHAR(25)  NOT NULL,
    model   VARCHAR(25)  NOT NULL,
    color   VARCHAR(25)
);

# insert 5 records into the "office_chairs" table
INSERT INTO steam_irons (make, model, color)
    VALUES ("Philips", "GC3020", "Lilac");
INSERT INTO steam_irons (make, model)
    VALUES ("Morphy Richards", "40608");
INSERT INTO steam_irons (make, model)
    VALUES ("Tefal", "1819 Avantis");
INSERT INTO steam_irons (make, model)
    VALUES ("Rowenta", "DM529");
INSERT INTO steam_irons (make, model, color)
    VALUES ("Bosch", "TDA8360", "Blue");

# show the table format
EXPLAIN steam_irons;

# show all data in the "steam_irons" table
SELECT * FROM steam_irons;
```

*filter-null.sql*
*(cont'd)*

```
# show all records where there is no specified color
SELECT * FROM steam_irons WHERE color IS NULL;

# delete this sample table
DROP TABLE IF EXISTS steam_irons;
```

The IS NULL keywords must be used to match NULL values in a SELECT query – using = NULL does not work.

Add the NOT keyword to an IS NULL clause to match where the tested field does contain a value – for instance, WHERE color IS NOT NULL.

```
 MySQL Command Line Client                              _ □ ✕

mysql> source C:\SQL\filter-null.sql
Database changed
Query OK, 0 rows affected (0.08 sec)

Query OK, 1 row affected (0.03 sec)

Query OK, 1 row affected (0.01 sec)

Query OK, 1 row affected (0.03 sec)

Query OK, 1 row affected (0.02 sec)

Query OK, 1 row affected (0.03 sec)

+-------+-------------+------+-----+---------+------
| Field | Type        | Null | Key | Default | Extr
+-------+-------------+------+-----+---------+------
| id    | int(11)     |      | PRI | NULL    | auto
| make  | varchar(25) |      |     |         |
| model | varchar(25) |      |     |         |
| color | varchar(25) | YES  |     | NULL    |
+-------+-------------+------+-----+---------+------
4 rows in set (0.00 sec)

+----+-----------------+--------------+-------+
| id | make            | model        | color |
+----+-----------------+--------------+-------+
|  1 | Philips         | GC3020       | Lilac |
|  2 | Morphy Richards | 40608        | NULL  |
|  3 | Tefal           | 1819 Avantis | NULL  |
|  4 | Rowenta         | DM529        | NULL  |
|  5 | Bosch           | TDA8360      | Blue  |
+----+-----------------+--------------+-------+
5 rows in set (0.00 sec)

+----+-----------------+--------------+-------+
| id | make            | model        | color |
+----+-----------------+--------------+-------+
|  2 | Morphy Richards | 40608        | NULL  |
|  3 | Tefal           | 1819 Avantis | NULL  |
|  4 | Rowenta         | DM529        | NULL  |
+----+-----------------+--------------+-------+
3 rows in set (0.00 sec)

Query OK, 0 rows affected (0.02 sec)

mysql> _
```

# Summary

- Specific data can be retrieved from a database table by stating search criteria in a SELECT query

- Search criteria are specified in the WHERE clause of a SELECT query

- Comparison operators are used to compare the contents of the fields in a particular column against a specified value

- A comparison is true when the evaluation succeeds and false when it fails

- The = equality operator evaluates a comparison as true when both values match

- The != inequality operator evaluates a comparison as true when the tested values do not match

- A > "greater than" operator evaluates a comparison as true when the tested column value exceeds the specified value

- A < "less than" operator evaluates a comparison as true when the tested column value is less than the specified value

- The <= and >= operators also evaluate comparisons as true when the tested column value matches the specified value

- A column value can be compared to a specified range of values with a BETWEEN AND clause

- Search criteria can test to see if column fields are empty with both IS NULL and IS NOT NULL clauses

- SQL comparison operators may vary from one DBMS to another – mostly adding to the basic comparison operators in this chapter

# Complex data filtering

This chapter builds on the previous one to introduce logical operators. These allow the WHERE clause in a SELECT query to stipulate multiple conditions for selecting data from a table. Examples also demonstrate how to use wildcards to search string data for specific substrings or character patterns.

## Covers

Chapter Eight

# Comparing multiple values

A WHERE clause in a SELECT query can make multiple comparisons using the AND logical operator. This enables comparisons to be made against the values contained in more than one column on each row. The syntax looks like this:

```
SELECT data FROM table-name
WHERE column = value AND column = value ;
```

The **WHERE** clause that states multiple expressions in this way will only evaluate as true when <u>all</u> comparisons evaluate as true.

In the following SQL script a SELECT query has a **WHERE** clause that makes two comparisons using the AND operator. The data is returned only for those rows that meet both conditions.

*filter-and.sql*
*(part of)*

```
# use the "my_database" database
USE my_database;

# create a table called "dining_sets"
CREATE TABLE IF NOT EXISTS dining_sets
(
    id          INT          AUTO_INCREMENT PRIMARY KEY,
    model       VARCHAR(25)  NOT NULL,
    color       VARCHAR(25)  NOT NULL,
    price       DECIMAL(6,2) NOT NULL
);

# insert 5 records into the "dining_sets" table
INSERT INTO dining_sets (model, color, price)
    VALUES ("Catalina", "Cherry", 349.99);
INSERT INTO dining_sets (model, color, price)
    VALUES ("Bistro", "Silver", 99.99);
INSERT INTO dining_sets (model, color, price)
    VALUES ("Michigan", "Silver", 179.99);
INSERT INTO dining_sets (model, color, price)
    VALUES ("Oregon", "Silver", 199.99);
INSERT INTO dining_sets (model, color, price)
    VALUES ("Medina", "Black", 159.99);
```

The WHERE query could state several comparisons with multiple AND operators – it is not limited to just two comparisons.

*filter-and.sql*
*(cont'd)*

```
# show all data in the "dining_sets" table
SELECT * FROM dining_sets;

# show all records where the color is "Silver"
# and the price is above 100.00
SELECT * FROM dining_sets
WHERE color = "Silver" AND price > 100.00;

# delete this sample table
DROP TABLE IF EXISTS dining_sets;
```

*In this example the "Bistro" data is not returned even though the "color" comparison is true, as "Silver" – the "price" comparison is false, being below 100.00.*

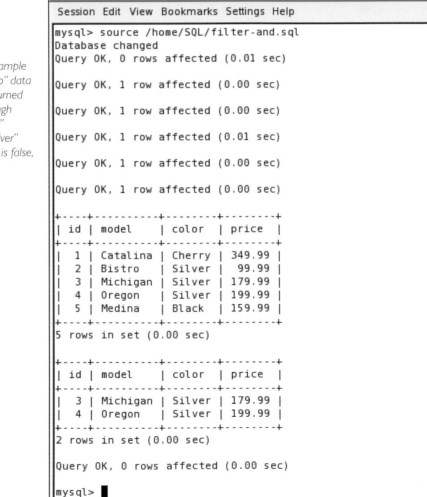

```
mysql> source /home/SQL/filter-and.sql
Database changed
Query OK, 0 rows affected (0.01 sec)

Query OK, 1 row affected (0.00 sec)

Query OK, 1 row affected (0.00 sec)

Query OK, 1 row affected (0.01 sec)

Query OK, 1 row affected (0.00 sec)

Query OK, 1 row affected (0.00 sec)

+----+----------+--------+--------+
| id | model    | color  | price  |
+----+----------+--------+--------+
|  1 | Catalina | Cherry | 349.99 |
|  2 | Bistro   | Silver |  99.99 |
|  3 | Michigan | Silver | 179.99 |
|  4 | Oregon   | Silver | 199.99 |
|  5 | Medina   | Black  | 159.99 |
+----+----------+--------+--------+
5 rows in set (0.00 sec)

+----+----------+--------+--------+
| id | model    | color  | price  |
+----+----------+--------+--------+
|  3 | Michigan | Silver | 179.99 |
|  4 | Oregon   | Silver | 199.99 |
+----+----------+--------+--------+
2 rows in set (0.00 sec)

Query OK, 0 rows affected (0.00 sec)

mysql>
```

# Comparing alternative values

A WHERE clause in a SELECT query can make multiple comparisons using the OR logical operator. This enables comparisons to be made against the values contained in more than one column on each row. The syntax looks like this:

```
SELECT data FROM table-name
WHERE column = value OR column = value ;
```

The **WHERE** clause that states multiple conditions in this way will evaluate as true when <u>any</u> of the comparisons evaluate as true.

The following SQL script builds the same table as the previous example but now a SELECT query has a WHERE clause that makes two comparisons using the OR operator. The data is returned only for those rows that meet any of the conditions.

*filter-or.sql*
*(part of)*

```
# use the "my_database" database
USE my_database;

# create a table called "dining_sets"
CREATE TABLE IF NOT EXISTS dining_sets
(
    id        INT           AUTO_INCREMENT PRIMARY KEY,
    model     VARCHAR(25)   NOT NULL,
    color     VARCHAR(25)   NOT NULL,
    price     DECIMAL(6,2)  NOT NULL
);

# insert 5 records into the "dining_sets" table
INSERT INTO dining_sets (model, color, price)
    VALUES ("Catalina", "Cherry", 349.99);
INSERT INTO dining_sets (model, color, price)
    VALUES ("Bistro", "Silver", 99.99);
INSERT INTO dining_sets (model, color, price)
    VALUES ("Michigan", "Silver", 179.99);
INSERT INTO dining_sets (model, color, price)
    VALUES ("Oregon", "Silver", 199.99);
INSERT INTO dining_sets (model, color, price)
    VALUES ("Medina", "Black", 159.99);
```

*The WHERE query could state several comparisons with multiple OR operators – it is not limited to just two comparisons.*

*filter-or.sql*
*(cont'd)*

```
# show all data in the "dining_sets" table
SELECT * FROM dining_sets;

# show all records where the color is not "Silver"
# or the price is below 100.00
SELECT * FROM dining_sets
WHERE color != "Silver" OR price < 100.00;

# delete this sample table
DROP TABLE IF EXISTS dining_sets;
```

*In this example the "Catalina" and "Medina" data is returned because the "color" comparison is true, they are not "Silver". The "Bistro" data is returned because the "price" comparison is true, being below 100.00.*

```
┌───────────────────────────────────────────────────────────┐
│ ⊛  Linux - Shell - Konsole              ▽ □ ⊗ │
├───────────────────────────────────────────────────────────┤
│ Session  Edit  View  Bookmarks  Settings  Help            │
├───────────────────────────────────────────────────────────┤
│ mysql> source /home/SQL/filter-or.sql              ▲      │
│ Database changed                                          │
│ Query OK, 0 rows affected (0.01 sec)                      │
│                                                           │
│ Query OK, 1 row affected (0.00 sec)                       │
│                                                           │
│ Query OK, 1 row affected (0.00 sec)                       │
│                                                           │
│ Query OK, 1 row affected (0.00 sec)                       │
│                                                           │
│ Query OK, 1 row affected (0.00 sec)                       │
│                                                           │
│ Query OK, 1 row affected (0.00 sec)                       │
│                                                           │
│ +----+----------+--------+--------+                       │
│ | id | model    | color  | price  |                       │
│ +----+----------+--------+--------+                       │
│ |  1 | Catalina | Cherry | 349.99 |                       │
│ |  2 | Bistro   | Silver |  99.99 |                       │
│ |  3 | Michigan | Silver | 179.99 |                       │
│ |  4 | Oregon   | Silver | 199.99 |                       │
│ |  5 | Medina   | Black  | 159.99 |                       │
│ +----+----------+--------+--------+                       │
│ 5 rows in set (0.00 sec)                                  │
│                                                           │
│ +----+----------+--------+--------+                       │
│ | id | model    | color  | price  |                       │
│ +----+----------+--------+--------+                       │
│ |  1 | Catalina | Cherry | 349.99 |                       │
│ |  2 | Bistro   | Silver |  99.99 |                       │
│ |  5 | Medina   | Black  | 159.99 |                       │
│ +----+----------+--------+--------+                       │
│ 3 rows in set (0.01 sec)                                  │
│                                                           │
│ Query OK, 0 rows affected (0.00 sec)               ▼      │
└───────────────────────────────────────────────────────────┘
```

# Comparing alternative lists

A WHERE clause in a SELECT query can specify a list of alternative values for comparison with column data using the IN keyword. This is followed by a comma-separated list of values within a single pair of parentheses. The syntax looks like this:

```
SELECT data FROM table-name
WHERE column IN ( value , value , value ) ;
```

When the column data matches any one of the values in the list, the WHERE clause evaluates as true and data is returned for that row. The comparison can be inverted by preceding the IN keyword with the NOT keyword. Then the WHERE clause only evaluates as true when no list value matches the column data.

The SQL script listed below demonstrates the comparison of multiple values using both IN and NOT IN clauses.

*filter-in.sql*
*(part of)*

```
# use the "my_database" database
USE my_database;

# create a table called "coffee_makers"
CREATE TABLE IF NOT EXISTS coffee_makers
(
    id          INT          AUTO_INCREMENT PRIMARY KEY,
    make        VARCHAR(25)  NOT NULL,
    model       VARCHAR(25)  NOT NULL,
    price       DECIMAL(6,2) NOT NULL
);

# insert 5 records into the "coffee_makers" table
INSERT INTO coffee_makers (make, model, price)
    VALUES ("Cookworks", "TSK-182", 19.99);
INSERT INTO coffee_makers (make, model, price)
    VALUES ("Morphy Richards", "Europa", 38.25);
INSERT INTO coffee_makers (make, model, price)
    VALUES ("Krups", "Vivo", 79.50);
INSERT INTO coffee_makers (make, model, price)
    VALUES ("DeLonghi", "EC410", 139.00);
INSERT INTO coffee_makers (make, model, price)
    VALUES ("Gaggia", "DeLuxe", 199.00);
```

*filter-in.sql*
*(cont'd)*

```
# show all data in the "coffee_makers" table
SELECT * FROM coffee_makers;

# show records where make is "Krups", "Gaggia" or
# "DeLonghi" and the model is not "TSK-182" or "EC410"
SELECT * FROM coffee_makers
WHERE make IN ("Krups", "Gaggia", "DeLonghi")
AND model NOT IN ("TSK-182", "EC410");

# delete this sample table
DROP TABLE IF EXISTS coffee_makers;
```

*In this example the "Krups", "Gaggia" and "DeLonghi" data is selected by the comparison to the first list. The second comparison list then excludes the "DeLonghi" data because its model value matches the second value in the comparison list.*

```
██ Linux - Shell - Konsole                         ▽ □ ⊗

Session Edit View Bookmarks Settings Help

mysql> source /home/SQL/filter-in.sql                  ▲
Database changed
Query OK, 0 rows affected (0.00 sec)

Query OK, 1 row affected (0.00 sec)

Query OK, 1 row affected (0.01 sec)

Query OK, 1 row affected (0.00 sec)

Query OK, 1 row affected (0.00 sec)

Query OK, 1 row affected (0.00 sec)

+----+-----------------+----------+--------+
| id | make            | model    | price  |
+----+-----------------+----------+--------+
|  1 | Cookworks       | TSK-182  |  19.99 |
|  2 | Morphy Richards | Europa   |  38.25 |
|  3 | Krups           | Vivo     |  79.50 |
|  4 | DeLonghi        | EC410    | 139.00 |
|  5 | Gaggia          | DeLuxe   | 199.00 |
+----+-----------------+----------+--------+
5 rows in set (0.00 sec)

+----+--------+--------+--------+
| id | make   | model  | price  |
+----+--------+--------+--------+
|  3 | Krups  | Vivo   |  79.50 |
|  5 | Gaggia | DeLuxe | 199.00 |
+----+--------+--------+--------+
2 rows in set (0.03 sec)

Query OK, 0 rows affected (0.00 sec)             ▼
```

# Specifying the evaluation order

The **WHERE** clause in a **SELECT** query can contain any number of comparison tests using the **AND** and **OR** keywords. But care must be taken in their use to avoid unexpected results which can be caused by the order in which the comparisons are evaluated.

The order of evaluation can be explicitly specified by surrounding an expression with parentheses – that expression then gets evaluated before anything else.

To demonstrate this problem, and its solution, the following script contains two **SELECT** queries that attempt to extract specific data. These two queries are identical except only one explicitly specifies the evaluation order. That one returns the correct data whereas the other one also returns a row of data erroneously.

*eval-order.sql*
*(part of)*

```
# use the "my_database" database
USE my_database;

# create a table called "backpacks"
CREATE TABLE IF NOT EXISTS backpacks
(
  id   INT   AUTO_INCREMENT PRIMARY KEY,
  make VARCHAR(8), model VARCHAR(25), price DECIMAL(6,2)
);

# insert 4 records into the "backpacks" table
INSERT INTO backpacks (make, model, price)
  VALUES ("Adidas", "NYC Uptown", 17.99);
INSERT INTO backpacks (make, model, price)
  VALUES ("Nike", "Arrow", 11.99);
INSERT INTO backpacks (make, model, price)
  VALUES ("Nike", "Sevilla", 13.99);
INSERT INTO backpacks (make, model, price)
  VALUES ("Reebok", "Streetsport", 11.99);

# show all data in the "backpacks" table
SELECT * FROM backpacks;

# show records where make is "Nike" or "Reebok"
# and price is 11.99 without explicit evaluation order
SELECT * FROM backpacks
WHERE make = "Nike"
OR make = "Reebok" AND price = 11.99;
```

*By default the AND operator takes precedence over the OR operator* – expressions using AND get evaluated first unless parentheses are used to explicitly specify an alternative order of precedence.

*eval-order.sql*
*(cont'd)*

```
# show records where make is "Nike" or "Reebok"
# and price is 11.99 with explicit evaluation order
SELECT * FROM backpacks
WHERE ( make = "Nike" OR make = "Reebok" )
AND price = 11.99;

# delete this sample table
DROP TABLE IF EXISTS backpacks;
```

```
Linux - Shell - Konsole

Session Edit View Bookmarks Settings Help

mysql> source /home/SQL/eval-order.sql
Database changed
Query OK, 0 rows affected (0.00 sec)

Query OK, 1 row affected (0.00 sec)

Query OK, 1 row affected (0.01 sec)

Query OK, 1 row affected (0.00 sec)

Query OK, 1 row affected (0.00 sec)

+----+--------+------------+-------+
| id | make   | model      | price |
+----+--------+------------+-------+
|  1 | Adidas | NYC Uptown | 17.99 |
|  2 | Nike   | Arrow      | 11.99 |
|  3 | Nike   | Sevilla    | 13.99 |
|  4 | Reebok | Streetsport| 11.99 |
+----+--------+------------+-------+
4 rows in set (0.00 sec)

+----+--------+------------+-------+
| id | make   | model      | price |
+----+--------+------------+-------+
|  2 | Nike   | Arrow      | 11.99 |
|  3 | Nike   | Sevilla    | 13.99 |
|  4 | Reebok | Streetsport| 11.99 |
+----+--------+------------+-------+
3 rows in set (0.00 sec)

+----+--------+------------+-------+
| id | make   | model      | price |
+----+--------+------------+-------+
|  2 | Nike   | Arrow      | 11.99 |
|  4 | Reebok | Streetsport| 11.99 |
+----+--------+------------+-------+
2 rows in set (0.00 sec)
```

*Always use parentheses to explicitly specify the evaluation order in any WHERE clause that includes both AND and OR keywords.*

# Matching strings

Making comparisons against text strings with the SQL comparison operators will only return data when the column's text data exactly matches the specified comparison text. This is not flexible and requires knowledge of the precise content of the column field.

The LIKE keyword offers an alternative way to make comparisons against text strings without requiring an exact complete match. This compares a "search pattern", comprising text and one or more wildcards, against the column string. Its syntax is like this:

```
SELECT data FROM table-name
WHERE column LIKE search-pattern ;
```

*Some DBMS', such as Access, use the "\*" character in place of the "%" wildcard.*

Each wildcard replaces part of the original string to allow comparison of just the text element. The most common wildcard is "%" which can precede and/or follow literal text to be compared. It matches zero, one or more characters at the point where it appears in the search pattern. For instance, "%red carpet%" could be used to match any compared column that contained the string "red carpet", regardless of any other text before or after that string.

The following SQL script creates a table populated with differing values in its "type" column. These are compared against a search pattern and the query returns data for the row whose compared column successfully matched against that search pattern.

*match-strings.sql*
*(part of)*

```
# use the "my_database" database
USE my_database;

# create a table called "shredders"
CREATE TABLE IF NOT EXISTS shredders
(
  model      VARCHAR(8)    PRIMARY KEY,
  type       VARCHAR(25)   DEFAULT "strip cut",
  price      DECIMAL(6,2)
);

# insert 4 records into the "shredders" table
INSERT INTO shredders (model, price)
  VALUES ("PS60", 64.99);
```

match-strings.sql
(cont'd)

```
INSERT INTO shredders (model, price)
  VALUES ("PS70", 99.99);
INSERT INTO shredders (model, type, price)
  VALUES ("PS400", "cross cut", 64.99);
INSERT INTO shredders (model, price)
  VALUES ("PS500", 29.95);

# show all data in the "shredders" table
SELECT * FROM shredders;

# show records where the model is a "cross cut" type
SELECT * FROM shredders WHERE type LIKE "%cross%";

# delete this sample table
DROP TABLE IF EXISTS shredders;
```

*Search patterns, like all other text strings, must be enclosed within quotes – including any wildcard characters.*

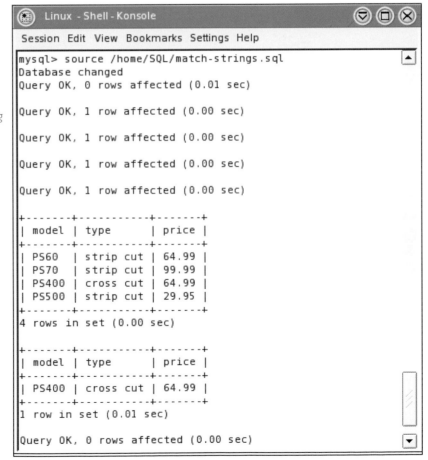

# Matching characters

The "%" wildcard represents zero, one, or more, characters in a search pattern. Another wildcard is the "_" underscore character that always represents just a single character in a search pattern.

The "_" wildcard is used in the same way as the "%" wildcard and can appear several times in a single search pattern to represent multiple characters. It can also be used alongside the "%" wildcard in a search pattern. For instance, the search pattern "t_b%" would seek to match any string beginning with a "t" whose third letter is "b" regardless of any following characters.

The following example uses the "_" wildcard to represent the third, fifth and sixth characters in a search pattern. These are compared with the string values in the table's "name" column – in this case there are two strings that match the search pattern.

*match-chars.sql*
*(part of)*

```
# use the "my_database" database
USE my_database;

# create a table called "glass_sets"
CREATE TABLE IF NOT EXISTS glass_sets
(
  id        INT          AUTO_INCREMENT PRIMARY KEY,
  name      VARCHAR(25)  NOT NULL,
  price     DECIMAL(6,2) NOT NULL
);
```

*Some DBMS, such as Access, use the "?" character in place of the "_" wildcard.*

```
# insert 5 records into the "glass_sets" table
INSERT INTO glass_sets (name, price)
  VALUES ("Monaco", 6.99);
INSERT INTO glass_sets (name, price)
  VALUES ("Cavendish", 4.99);
INSERT INTO glass_sets (name, price)
  VALUES ("Mosaic", 6.99);
INSERT INTO glass_sets (name, price)
  VALUES ("Blue Reef", 8.99);
INSERT INTO glass_sets (name, price)
  VALUES ("Silver Swirl", 14.99);

# show all data in the "glass_sets" table
SELECT * FROM glass_sets;
```

*match-chars.sql*
*(cont'd)*

```
# show records where the name matches a search pattern
SELECT * FROM glass_sets WHERE name LIKE "mo_a__";
```

```
Linux - Shell - Konsole

Session  Edit  View  Bookmarks  Settings  Help

mysql> source /home/SQL/match-chars.sql
Database changed
Query OK, 0 rows affected (0.01 sec)

Query OK, 1 row affected (0.00 sec)

Query OK, 1 row affected (0.00 sec)

Query OK, 1 row affected (0.00 sec)

Query OK, 1 row affected (0.01 sec)

Query OK, 1 row affected (0.00 sec)

+----+--------------+-------+
| id | name         | price |
+----+--------------+-------+
|  1 | Monaco       |  6.99 |
|  2 | Cavendish    |  4.99 |
|  3 | Mosaic       |  6.99 |
|  4 | Blue Reef    |  8.99 |
|  5 | Silver Swirl | 14.99 |
+----+--------------+-------+
5 rows in set (0.00 sec)

+----+--------+-------+
| id | name   | price |
+----+--------+-------+
|  1 | Monaco |  6.99 |
|  3 | Mosaic |  6.99 |
+----+--------+-------+
2 rows in set (0.00 sec)

mysql> █
```

*Remember that the "_" wildcard always matches exactly one character.*

This SQL example does not delete the "glass_sets" table so it can be used to demonstrate further comparison queries by the example on the next page.

# Matching regular expressions

Powerful search patterns can be specified as "regular expressions" using the REGEXP keyword. These can add special characters to text in the search pattern to signify their significance. The table below contains some common examples of regular expressions.

| Regular Expression | Matches |
| --- | --- |
| "A" | A single character – here it's any string containing a letter A |
| "[ABC]" | A list of characters – here it's any string containing one of the letters A or B or C |
| "[A-K]" | A range of characters – here it's any string containing one of the letters A through K |
| "[0-5]" | A range of digits – here it's any string containing one of the digits 0 through 5 |
| "^M" | A single character at the beginning of the string – here it's any string starting with the letter M |
| "H$" | A single character at the end of the string – here it's any string ending with the letter H |

*Support for regular expressions does vary from one DBMS to another. In MySQL they are not case sensitive – so the expression "A" would match any string containing a letter "A" in either uppercase or lowercase.*

The following SQL script queries the "glass_sets" table that was created in the previous example. It matches a number of regular expressions to strings contained in the "name" column.

*match-regexp.sql*
*(part of)*

```
# show records where the name contains a "W"
SELECT * FROM glass_sets WHERE name REGEXP "W";

# show records where the name contains a "W" or a "N"
SELECT * FROM glass_sets WHERE name REGEXP "[WN]";

# show records where the name begins with a "B"
SELECT * FROM glass_sets WHERE name REGEXP "^B";

# show records where the name ends with a "H"
SELECT * FROM glass_sets WHERE name REGEXP "H$";
```

*match-regexp.sql*
*(cont'd)*

```
# show records where the name begins with a "B" or "C"
SELECT * FROM glass_sets WHERE name REGEXP "^[BC]";

# now delete this sample table
DROP TABLE IF EXISTS glass_sets;
```

*Single characters can be matched in a regular expression by a dot. For instance, "^....$" would match any string that contains exactly four characters.*

*Put the NOT keyword before the REGEXP keyword to return all strings that don't match the expression.*

```
Linux - Shell - Konsole

Session  Edit  View  Bookmarks  Settings  Help

mysql> source /home/SQL/match-regexp.sql
+----+-------------+-------+
| id | name        | price |
+----+-------------+-------+
|  5 | Silver Swirl | 14.99 |
+----+-------------+-------+
1 row in set (0.03 sec)

+----+-------------+-------+
| id | name        | price |
+----+-------------+-------+
|  1 | Monaco      |  6.99 |
|  2 | Cavendish   |  4.99 |
|  5 | Silver Swirl | 14.99 |
+----+-------------+-------+
3 rows in set (0.00 sec)

+----+-----------+-------+
| id | name      | price |
+----+-----------+-------+
|  4 | Blue Reef |  8.99 |
+----+-----------+-------+
1 row in set (0.00 sec)

+----+-----------+-------+
| id | name      | price |
+----+-----------+-------+
|  2 | Cavendish |  4.99 |
+----+-----------+-------+
1 row in set (0.01 sec)

+----+-----------+-------+
| id | name      | price |
+----+-----------+-------+
|  2 | Cavendish |  4.99 |
|  4 | Blue Reef |  8.99 |
+----+-----------+-------+
2 rows in set (0.00 sec)

Query OK, 0 rows affected (0.00 sec)
```

# Summary

- The logical AND operator can be added to a WHERE clause in a SELECT query to allow comparisons against multiple columns

- All multiple AND comparisons must evaluate as true in order for the WHERE clause to return data from the current row

- The logical OR operator can be added to a WHERE clause in a SELECT query to allow comparisons against multiple columns

- Any one of the multiple OR comparisons must evaluate as true in order for the WHERE clause to return data from the current row

- A WHERE clause can specify a comma-separated list of alternative comparison values in parentheses following the IN keyword

- Data can be returned from rows that do <u>not</u> match any of the list of values by adding a NOT keyword before the IN keyword

- Both logical AND and OR operators can be added to a single WHERE clause to allow comparisons against multiple columns

- The AND operator is evaluated before the OR operator

- Parentheses should be added to WHERE clauses that contain both AND and OR operators to specify the evaluation order

- The LIKE operator can be added to a WHERE clause to specify a search pattern for comparison against a string value

- A "%" wildcard represents zero, one or more, characters in a search pattern

- A "_" wildcard represents just one character in a search pattern

- Search patterns may contain multiple instances of the "%" and "_" wildcards

- The REGEXP keyword can be used in a WHERE clause to specify a regular expression for comparison against a string value

- Data can be returned from rows that do <u>not</u> match a regular expression using the NOT REGEXP keywords

# Generating calculated fields

This chapter introduces the topic of "calculated fields" within a database table. It begins by explaining what a calculated field is and how it can be useful. Examples demonstrate how they are created and how to use aliases to label them.

## Covers

**Chapter Nine**

# Concatenating fields

A "calculated field" is created using data stored within several columns of a database. It does not form an additional column in the table but is generated dynamically to display the result of a calculation that uses data from existing fields.

Calculated fields are useful to present a range of data in a formatted manner. For instance, a table may typically store address data in separate columns for street, city, state and zip code, but a mailing program needs this data to be retrieved as a single formatted field. This requires the data stored in the various columns to be concatenated (joined together) to form a single calculated field.

*Consult the documentation of your DBMS to discover which type of concatenation it supports.*

The technique to concatenate string data varies by DBMS, but usually a formatting separator is placed between each piece of data. This typically may be a space, comma or newline character.

Some DBMS', such as those from Microsoft, favor concatenation using the "+" operator, with this syntax:

> *calculated-field = column1 + separator + column2*

The "+" operator in this case recognizes the column data type as text so it attempts to concatenate the strings – rather than attempt a numerical addition. Other databases, such as Oracle, favor the "||" operator for concatenation in place of the "+" character.

MySQL has a special CONCAT keyword for this purpose that allows the columns to be concatenated to be specified as a comma-separated list within parentheses after this keyword. For concatenation with a designated separator it also has a similar CONCAT_WS keyword that automatically recognizes the first item in the list as a separator to include between each piece of data. The syntax for this concatenation feature looks like this:

*CONCAT_WS means "Concatenate With Separator"*

> *CONCAT_WS ( separator , column1 , column2 )*

The SQL script on the opposite page demonstrates the creation of calculated fields with both CONCAT and CONCAT_WS.

*concat.sql*

```
# use the "my_database" database
USE my_database;

# create a table called "hotels"
CREATE TABLE IF NOT EXISTS hotels
(
  name VARCHAR(25) PRIMARY KEY, street VARCHAR(25),
  city VARCHAR(25), state VARCHAR(25), zip INT
);

# insert a record into the "hotels" table
INSERT INTO hotels (name, street, city, state, zip)
  VALUES ("Las Vegas Hilton", "3000 Paradise Road",
          "Las Vegas", "Nevada", 89109);

# retrieve 2 concatenated calculated fields
SELECT CONCAT(name, ", ", state) FROM hotels;
SELECT CONCAT_WS(",\n", name, street, city, state, zip)
FROM hotels;

# delete this sample table
DROP TABLE IF EXISTS hotels;
```

*In this example, CONCAT adds a comma and a space separator whereas CONCAT_WS adds a comma and a "\n" newline separator between each item of data.*

```
MySQL Command Line Client                          _ □ ✕

mysql> source C:\SQL\concat.sql
Database changed
Query OK, 0 rows affected (0.09 sec)

Query OK, 1 row affected (0.02 sec)

+---------------------------+
| CONCAT(name, ", ", state) |
+---------------------------+
| Las Vegas Hilton, Nevada  |
+---------------------------+
1 row in set (0.00 sec)


+-------------------------------------------------------+
| CONCAT_WS(",\n", name, street, city, state, zip)      |
+-------------------------------------------------------+
| Las Vegas Hilton,
3000 Paradise Road,
Las Vegas,
Nevada,
89109 |
+-------------------------------------------------------+
1 row in set (0.00 sec)

Query OK, 0 rows affected (0.04 sec)
```

# Trimming padding spaces

Some databases automatically add spaces to strings to pad them out to the column width. For instance, with a column data type of **VARCHAR(10)**, a five-letter string might have five trailing spaces added to pad it out to the full column width.

Padded strings do not usually present a problem when retrieving single items of data, but they are not desirable when concatenating several strings into a calculated field.

All leading and trailing spaces can be removed from a string with the **TRIM** keyword. The name of the column to be trimmed should follow this keyword within parentheses, like this:

```
TRIM ( column )
```

Most DBMS' also support **LTRIM** and **RTRIM** keywords which trim spaces from the left and right of the string respectively.

MySQL does not automatically pad strings with spaces to the column width, but strings that are stored with leading and/or trailing spaces can be trimmed with the **TRIM** keyword.

The following example SQL script creates a table populated with string values that deliberately have both leading and trailing spaces. The strings are trimmed by each **SELECT** query to return concatenated calculated fields.

*trim.sql*
*(part of)*

```
# use the "my_database" database
USE my_database;

# create a table called "padded"
CREATE TABLE IF NOT EXISTS padded
(
  id  INT    AUTO_INCREMENT PRIMARY KEY,
  str1 CHAR(10), str2 CHAR(10), str3 CHAR(10)
);

# insert 2 records into the "padded" table
INSERT INTO padded (str1, str2, str3)
  VALUES (" MySQL    ", " Data    ", " Bases    ");
```

*trim.sql*
*(cont'd)*

```sql
INSERT INTO padded (str1, str2, str3)
  VALUES (" are      ", " great    ", " fun !    ");

# show all data in the "padded" table
SELECT * FROM padded;

# retrieve 2 trimmed concatenated calculated fields
SELECT CONCAT( TRIM(str1), RTRIM(str2), LTRIM(str3) )
FROM padded WHERE id = 1;

SELECT CONCAT( TRIM(str1), RTRIM(str2), TRIM(str3) )
FROM padded WHERE id = 2;

# delete this sample table
DROP TABLE IF EXISTS padded;
```

*This example uses a combination of TRIM, LTRIM and RTRIM to format the strings as required.*

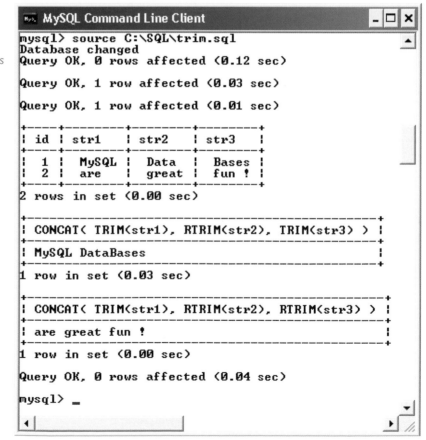

# Using aliases

In the previous examples in this chapter the heading of each calculated field simply displays the code that created that field. It is often preferable to assign a meaningful heading to label the calculated field instead – in the same way that a column header labels a regular column. This label is known as an "alias" and is specified by the AS keyword in a SELECT query.

If an alias is to include spaces it should be enclosed within quotes when specified by the AS keyword – a single word alias does not need quotes around it.

The following SQL script creates and populates a table then generates two calculated fields, each labeled with an alias. Note that the EXPLAIN query confirms that the calculated field is only generated as output and is not actually added to the table.

*alias.sql*
*(part of)*

```
# use the "my_database" database
USE my_database;

# create a table called "fishermans_wharf"
CREATE TABLE IF NOT EXISTS fishermans_wharf
(
    street      VARCHAR(20)   PRIMARY KEY,
    city        CHAR(20)      DEFAULT "San Francisco",
    state       CHAR(2)       DEFAULT "CA",
    zip         INT           DEFAULT 94133
);
```

*Aliases can also be used to dynamically replace a column header in output. This does not change the name given to the column – only the label in the SELECT query response output.*

```
# insert 2 records into the "fishermans_wharf" table
INSERT INTO fishermans_wharf (street)
    VALUES ("145 Jefferson St.");
INSERT INTO fishermans_wharf (street)
    VALUES ("175 Jefferson St.");

# show all data in the "fishermans_wharf" table
SELECT * FROM fishermans_wharf;

# retrieve 2 concatenated calculated fields
SELECT CONCAT_WS(", ", street, city, state, zip)
AS Wax_Museum
FROM fishermans_wharf
WHERE street = "145 Jefferson St.";
```

*alias.sql*
*(cont'd)*

```
SELECT CONCAT_WS(", ", street, city, state, zip)
AS "Ripley's Believe It Or Not! Museum"
FROM fishermans_wharf
WHERE street = "175 Jefferson St.";

# display the table format
EXPLAIN fishermans_wharf;

# delete this sample table
DROP TABLE IF EXISTS fishermans_wharf;
```

```
MySQL Command Line Client                                    _ □ ×

mysql> source C:\SQL\alias.sql
Database changed
Query OK, 0 rows affected (0.07 sec)

Query OK, 1 row affected (0.02 sec)

Query OK, 1 row affected (0.04 sec)

+------------------+---------------+-------+-------+
| street           | city          | state | zip   |
+------------------+---------------+-------+-------+
| 145 Jefferson St.| San Francisco | CA    | 94133 |
| 175 Jefferson St.| San Francisco | CA    | 94133 |
+------------------+---------------+-------+-------+
2 rows in set (0.00 sec)

+-------------------------------------------------+
| Wax_Museum                                      |
+-------------------------------------------------+
| 145 Jefferson St., San Francisco, CA, 94133     |
+-------------------------------------------------+
1 row in set (0.00 sec)

+-------------------------------------------------+
| Ripley's Believe It Or Not! Museum              |
+-------------------------------------------------+
| 175 Jefferson St., San Francisco, CA, 94133     |
+-------------------------------------------------+
1 row in set (0.00 sec)

+--------+-------------+------+-----+---------------+
| Field  | Type        | Null | Key | Default       |
+--------+-------------+------+-----+---------------+
| street | varchar(20) |      | PRI |               |
| city   | varchar(20) | YES  |     | San Francisco |
| state  | char(2)     | YES  |     | CA            |
| zip    | int(11)     | YES  |     | 94133         |
+--------+-------------+------+-----+---------------+
4 rows in set (0.01 sec)

Query OK, 0 rows affected (0.03 sec)
```

Aliases that contain strings can sometimes cause problems in certain client applications. Although legal, it is better to use single word aliases or to link the words with the underscore character – as seen in this example.

# Making arithmetical calculations

Perhaps the most useful aspect of calculated fields is to perform arithmetical operations on existing data and present the result of the calculation in a newly generated field. SQL provides the standard arithmetical operators, listed in the table below:

| | |
|---|---|
| + | Addition |
| – | Subtraction |
| * | Multiplication |
| / | Division |

This SQL script example uses arithmetical operators to calculate data to be entered into calculated fields. It first creates a table then populates two of its columns with numerical data for "price" and "quantity".

The SELECT query in this example generates a calculated field, named "subtotal", to store the result of multiplying the price and quantity values on each row. It also generates a second calculated field, named "tax", to store the result of multiplying the subtotal on each row by 6%. A third calculated field, named "total", stores the result of adding the "subtotal" and "tax" on each row to produce a grand total.

*calculate.sql*
*(part of)*

```
# use the "my_database" database
USE my_database;

# create a table called "wines"
CREATE TABLE IF NOT EXISTS wines
(
    id        INT     AUTO_INCREMENT      PRIMARY KEY,
    type      CHAR(10)     NOT NULL,
    price     DECIMAL(6,2) NOT NULL,
    quantity  INT          DEFAULT 0
);
```

*calculate.sql*
*(cont'd)*

```
# insert 3 records into the "wines" table
INSERT INTO wines (type, price, quantity)
  VALUES ("Red", 10.00, 12);

INSERT INTO wines (type, price, quantity)
  VALUES ("White", 9.00, 12);

INSERT INTO wines (type, price, quantity)
  VALUES ("Rose", 8.00, 6);

# generate calculated fields
SELECT      type,
            price AS bottle,
            quantity AS qty,
            price * quantity AS subtotal,
            (price * quantity) * (6 / 100) AS tax,
            (price * quantity) +
            (price * quantity) * (6 / 100) AS total
FROM wines ;

# delete this sample table
DROP TABLE wines;
```

*In this example the "quantity" column has been given the alias of "qty" just to reduce that column's width – so that the complete output from the SELECT query would fit in the screenshot.*

```
MySQL Command Line Client                         _ □ ✕

mysql> source C:\SQL\calculate.sql
Database changed
Query OK, 0 rows affected (0.11 sec)

Query OK, 1 row affected (0.03 sec)

Query OK, 1 row affected (0.01 sec)

Query OK, 1 row affected (0.03 sec)

+-------+--------+-----+----------+------+--------+
| type  | bottle | qty | subtotal | tax  | total  |
+-------+--------+-----+----------+------+--------+
| Red   |  10.00 |  12 |   120.00 | 7.20 | 127.20 |
| White |   9.00 |  12 |   108.00 | 6.48 | 114.48 |
| Rose  |   8.00 |   6 |    48.00 | 2.88 |  50.88 |
+-------+--------+-----+----------+------+--------+
3 rows in set (0.00 sec)

Query OK, 0 rows affected (0.02 sec)

mysql> _
```

# Summary

- A "calculated field" is generated dynamically to display the result of a calculation that uses data from existing fields

- Multiple strings can be concatenated into one single string

- The methods of concatenating strings varies according to the DBMS specifications

- Some DBMS' use the "+" operator for concatenation, others use the "||" operator

- MySQL uses special CONCAT and CONCAT_WS keywords for concatenating strings

- The strings to be concatenated are specified as a comma-separated list within parentheses after the CONCAT or CONCAT_WS keywords

- CONCAT_WS recognizes the first item in its specified list as a separator that it automatically inserts between each string

- Trailing and leading spaces can be removed from strings with the TRIM, LTRIM and RTRIM keywords

- An alias is a meaningful label that is assigned to a calculated field using the AS keyword in a SELECT query

- The regular column heading can be replaced by an alias in the output from a SELECT query

- Arithmetical operations can be performed on numerical data using the "+","-","*" and "/" arithmetical operators

- The result of arithmetical operations on existing data can usefully be displayed in a newly generated calculated field

# Manipulating data

This chapter introduces SQL functions that allow data to be converted and manipulated. Examples demonstrate how to manipulate text strings, dates, numbers and data types.

## Covers

**Chapter Ten**

# Introducing functions

An SQL function is a keyword that performs a particular pre-ordained operation on a specified piece of data. The data is specified within parentheses following the keyword. This may be a single item or a comma-separated list – depending on the nature of the function. These are known as the function "arguments".

In the previous chapter CONCAT(), CONCAT_WS(), TRIM(), RTRIM() and LTRIM() are all SQL functions – each performing a particular task on the data specified within their parentheses.

The four types of SQL functions are listed in the following table together with a description of what they do.

| | |
|---|---|
| Text functions | Used to manipulate strings of text. For instance, trimming spaces and converting to uppercase or lowercase |
| Numeric functions | Used to perform mathematical operations. For instance, returning an absolute value or calculating an algebraic expression |
| Date functions | Used to manipulate date and time values. For instance, returning the current time and calculating the difference between two dates |
| System functions | Used to return information about the DBMS itself. For instance, the version number, user information and connection number |

All DBMS' provide SQL functions for the most useful operations but, unfortunately, the function names and syntax vary from one DBMS to another. This means that SQL code containing function calls is not portable between various DBMS'.

The following table lists some common function operations together with their relevant function names on some of the most popular DBMS'.

| Operation | Oracle | SQL Server | MySQL |
|---|---|---|---|
| Return part of a string | SUBSTR() | SUBSTRING() | SUBSTRING() |
| Convert a data type | TO_CHAR() TO_NUMBER() | CONVERT() | CONVERT() |
| Return a rounded-up number | CEIL() | CEILING() | CEILING() |
| Return the current date | SYSDATE | GETDATE() | CURDATE() |

Because of these differences some programmers opt to avoid SQL functions in favor of having their program perform the required operation on the data. This enables the program to be portable across various DBMS', but is generally less efficient.

SQL functions within a DBMS are optimized for maximum efficiency and should be used wherever possible rather than have an application perform the required operation.

The examples in the rest of this chapter feature SQL functions which are supported by MySQL. For other DBMS' the equivalent function name and syntax must be substituted – refer to the documentation for your DBMS to discover the equivalent function name and syntax in each case.

# Text functions

A section of textual data can be extracted with the SUBSTRING() function. This requires three arguments to be specified within its parentheses – stating the string, the character position at which to begin the substring and the length of the substring. Its syntax is:

SUBSTRING ( *string* , *position* , *length* )

*Function names and syntax do vary on different DBMS' – see the documentation of your DBMS for its supported functions.*

A string can be returned in uppercase with the UPPER() function, or in lowercase with the LOWER() function. The number of characters in a string can be returned using the LENGTH() function. String data values which sound similar can be returned using the SOUNDEX() function. This uses an algorithm to return an alphanumeric pattern that is a phonetic representation of the string. The pattern allows for characters and syllables that sound alike – so strings may be compared by how they sound, rather than how they are written. Each of these functions just require the string to be specified within its parentheses.

The following SQL script example returns substrings, uppercase and lowercase versions, string lengths and patterns.

*str-fcn.sql
(part of)*

```
USE my_database;     # use the "my_database" database

# create a table called "party"
CREATE TABLE IF NOT EXISTS party
(
  id        INT    AUTO_INCREMENT PRIMARY KEY,
  dept      CHAR(10),     name CHAR(25)
);

# insert 3 records into the "party" table
INSERT INTO party (dept, name)
  VALUES ("accounts", "Graham Miller");
INSERT INTO party (dept, name)
  VALUES ("sales", "Gary Miller");
INSERT INTO party (dept, name)
  VALUES ("production", "Graham Wallace");

# get 3-letter substrings from the dept column
SELECT SUBSTRING(dept, 1, 3) FROM party
```

*str-fcn.sql*
*(cont'd)*

```
# get both cases name and length in the production dept
SELECT UPPER(name), LOWER(name), LENGTH(name)
FROM party WHERE dept = "production";

# get pattern and names that sound like "Gary Miller"
SELECT SOUNDEX(name), name FROM party
WHERE SOUNDEX(name) = SOUNDEX("Gary Miller");

# delete this sample table
DROP TABLE IF EXISTS party;
```

```
┌─────────────────────────────────────────────────────────────┐
│  (*)   Linux - Shell - Konsole          ⊽ □ ⊗              │
├─────────────────────────────────────────────────────────────┤
│  Session  Edit  View  Bookmarks  Settings  Help             │
├─────────────────────────────────────────────────────────────┤
│ mysql> source /home/SQL/str-fcn.sql                      ▲  │
│ Database changed                                            │
│ Query OK, 0 rows affected (0.02 sec)                       │
│                                                            │
│ Query OK, 1 row affected (0.01 sec)                        │
│                                                            │
│ Query OK, 1 row affected (0.00 sec)                        │
│                                                            │
│ Query OK, 1 row affected (0.00 sec)                        │
│                                                            │
│ +----------------------+                                   │
│ | SUBSTRING(dept, 1, 3) |                                  │
│ +----------------------+                                   │
│ | acc                  |                                   │
│ | sal                  |                                   │
│ | pro                  |                                   │
│ +----------------------+                                   │
│ 3 rows in set (0.01 sec)                                   │
│                                                            │
│ +---------------+----------------+---------------+         │
│ | UPPER(name)   | LOWER(name)    | LENGTH(name)  |         │
│ +---------------+----------------+---------------+         │
│ | GRAHAM WALLACE | graham wallace |            14 |        │
│ +---------------+----------------+---------------+         │
│ 1 row in set (0.01 sec)                                    │
│                                                            │
│ +---------------+----------------+                         │
│ | SOUNDEX(name) | name           |                         │
│ +---------------+----------------+                         │
│ | G6546         | Graham Miller  |                         │
│ | G6546         | Gary Miller    |                         │
│ +---------------+----------------+                         │
│ 2 rows in set (0.00 sec)                                   │
│                                                            │
│ Query OK, 0 rows affected (0.00 sec)                    ▼  │
└─────────────────────────────────────────────────────────────┘
```

*Notice that the SOUNDEX() pattern is identical for both these names.*

# Numeric functions

SQL provides a number of standard functions for mathematical calculation – these are generally standard on all DBMS'. Some of the most useful math functions are listed in the table below:

*Some DBMS' support other Math functions in addition to those listed here – refer to the documentation for your DBMS to discover them.*

| Function | Returns |
|----------|---------|
| ABS($x$) | Absolute value of $x$ |
| COS($x$) | Cosine of $x$, where $x$ is given in radians |
| EXP($x$) | Exponential value of $x$ |
| MOD($x$ , $y$) | Remainder of $x$ divided by $y$ |
| PI() | 3.141593 |
| RADIANS($x$) | Degrees $x$ converted to radians |
| SIN($x$) | Sine of $x$ where $x$ is given in radians |
| SQRT($x$) | Square root of $x$ |
| TAN($x$) | Tangent of $x$ where $x$ is given in radians |
| FLOOR($x$) | Nearest integer value below $x$ |
| CEILING($x$) | Nearest integer value above $x$ |
| ROUND($x$) | Nearest integer above or below $x$ |
| RAND() | Random number in the range 0 to 1.0 |

The modulus function, MOD(), is useful to determine if a specified value is odd or even – dividing the value by 2 returns 1 for odd numbers and zero for even numbers.

Floating-point numbers can easily be rounded up to the nearest integer with the CEILING() function, or rounded down to the nearest integer with the FLOOR() function.

The example SQL script on the opposite page demonstrates some of the above functions in action and illustrates how the random floating-point value returned by the RAND() function can be translated to a more useful integer value in the range of 1 to 100.

*math-fcn.sql*

```
# get some square roots
SELECT SQRT(144), SQRT(125), ROUND(SQRT(125));

# get Pi and round it up and down
SELECT PI(), CEILING(PI()), FLOOR(PI());

# get some random numbers
SELECT RAND(), RAND();

# get some random numbers in the range 1-100
SELECT CEILING(RAND() * 100), CEILING(RAND() * 100);
```

```
Linux - Shell - Konsole

Session  Edit  View  Bookmarks  Settings  Help

mysql> source /home/SQL/math-fcn.sql
+-----------+-----------------+-----------------+
| SQRT(144) | SQRT(125)       | ROUND(SQRT(125)) |
+-----------+-----------------+-----------------+
|        12 | 11.180339887499 |              11 |
+-----------+-----------------+-----------------+
1 row in set (0.00 sec)

+----------+-------------+------------+
| pi()     | CEILING(PI()) | FLOOR(PI()) |
+----------+-------------+------------+
| 3.141593 |           4 |          3 |
+----------+-------------+------------+
1 row in set (0.00 sec)

+------------------+------------------+
| RAND()           | RAND()           |
+------------------+------------------+
| 0.28007921788849 | 0.59311357288911 |
+------------------+------------------+
1 row in set (0.00 sec)

+--------------------+--------------------+
| CEILING(RAND() * 100) | CEILING(RAND() * 100) |
+--------------------+--------------------+
|                 13 |                 85 |
+--------------------+--------------------+
1 row in set (0.00 sec)

mysql>
```

# Date and time functions

Dates and times are stored in SQL database tables as DATE, TIME or DATETIME data types. These have specific formats to store the seconds, minutes, hours, day, month and year components of a date and time in an ordered manner.

*Refer back to the data type table on page 38 for date and time formats.*

Each component of a stored date or time can be retrieved individually using an SQL function that specifies the date or time within its parentheses. SECOND(), MINUTE() and HOUR() return the relevant time components. DAYOFMONTH(), MONTHNAME() and YEAR() return the relevant date components. Additionally the day's name can be returned with the DAYNAME() function.

The full current data and time can be returned with the NOW() function. The current date can be returned by the CURDATE() function and the current time by the CURTIME() function.

This example first returns the current date and time information. It then retrieves the individual date and time components from a DATETIME data type in the format YYYY-MM-DD HH:MM:SS.

*date-fcn.sql*
*(part of)*

```
# get the current full date object, current date & time
SELECT NOW(), CURDATE(), CURTIME();

# use the my_database database
USE my_database;

# create a table called "labor_day"
CREATE TABLE IF NOT EXISTS labor_day
(
    id      INT          AUTO_INCREMENT PRIMARY KEY,
    date    DATETIME     NOT NULL
);

# insert 1 record into the "labor_day" table
INSERT INTO labor_day (date)
VALUES ("2005-09-05 12:45:30");

# get the name of the day
SELECT DAYNAME(date) FROM labor_day;
```

*Date and time functions vary greatly on different DBMS' – see the documentation of your DBMS for its date and time functions.*

*date-fcn.sql*
*(cont'd)*

```
# get the day, month and year date components
SELECT DAYOFMONTH(date), MONTHNAME(date),YEAR(date)
FROM labor_day;

# get the hour, minute and second time components
SELECT HOUR(date), MINUTE(date), SECOND(date)
FROM labor_day;

# delete this sample table
DROP TABLE IF EXISTS labor_day;
```

*Use the BETWEEN and AND keywords to match a range of dates.*

*There is also a MONTH() function that returns the month number in the range of 1 – 12.*

```
Linux - Shell - Konsole

Session  Edit  View  Bookmarks  Settings  Help

mysql> source /home/SQL/date-fcn.sql
+---------------------+-----------+-----------+
| NOW()               | CURDATE() | CURTIME() |
+---------------------+-----------+-----------+
| 2005-03-13 17:55:25 | 2005-03-13 | 17:55:25 |
+---------------------+-----------+-----------+
1 row in set (0.03 sec)

Database changed
Query OK, 0 rows affected (0.03 sec)

Query OK, 1 row affected (0.00 sec)

+---------------+
| DAYNAME(date) |
+---------------+
| Monday        |
+---------------+
1 row in set (0.00 sec)

+------------------+-----------------+------------+
| DAYOFMONTH(date) | MONTHNAME(date) | YEAR(date) |
+------------------+-----------------+------------+
|                5 | September       |       2005 |
+------------------+-----------------+------------+
1 row in set (0.00 sec)

+------------+--------------+--------------+
| HOUR(date) | MINUTE(date) | SECOND(date) |
+------------+--------------+--------------+
|         12 |           45 |           30 |
+------------+--------------+--------------+
1 row in set (0.03 sec)

Query OK, 0 rows affected (0.00 sec)
```

# System functions

MySQL provides a number of SQL functions and keywords to administer the database system internally. The VERSION() function simply returns the version number of the DBMS and the USER() function displays the name and domain of the user.

Log into MySQL as the root user, or as a user with all privileges, to be allowed to make GRANT statements.

Type "quit" to logout of the MySQL monitor, then type "mysql -u root" to log back in as root.

Each access to the database runs in an individual process known as a "thread". The SHOW PROCESSLIST statement will reveal the identity number of each thread. Any individual thread can be terminated by specifying its identity number within the parentheses of the KILL() function.

New database users can be added with a GRANT statement that specifies their level of activity privileges. A typical GRANT statement that adds a new user with password-required access and full privileges looks like this:

```
GRANT ALL PRIVILEGES ON *.* TO monty@localhost
IDENTIFIED BY "password" WITH GRANT OPTION ;
```

*Each DBMS can set a wide range of specific privileges for a user – please refer to your DBMS documentation for full details.*

The level of privileges granted to a user can be inspected with a SHOW GRANTS FOR statement, specifiying the user name.

The SQL script below first displays the MySQL version number and current user. It then creates a new user with password access and full privileges. The new user can now connect to the MySQL DBMS using the specified name and password.

*sys-fcn.sql*

```
# get the version number and current user
SELECT VERSION(), USER();

# get the thread identity
SHOW PROCESSLIST;

# create a new user with full privileges
GRANT ALL PRIVILEGES ON *.* TO monty@localhost
IDENTIFIED BY "password" WITH GRANT OPTION;

# confirm privileges for the new user
SHOW GRANTS FOR monty@localhost;
```

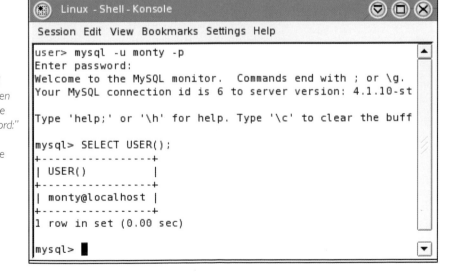

```
 ┌──────────────────────────────────────────────────────────────────┐
 │ ⊛  Linux - Shell - Konsole                        ▽ ▢ ⊗           │
 ├──────────────────────────────────────────────────────────────────┤
 │ Session  Edit  View  Bookmarks  Settings  Help                   │
 ├──────────────────────────────────────────────────────────────────┤
 │ mysql> source /home/SQL/sys-fcn.sql                         ▲    │
 │ +-----------------+-----------------+                            │
 │ | VERSION()       | USER()          |                            │
 │ +-----------------+-----------------+                            │
 │ | 4.1.10-standard | root@localhost  |                            │
 │ +-----------------+-----------------+                            │
 │ 1 row in set (0.00 sec)                                          │
 │                                                                  │
 │ +----+------+-----------+------+---------+------+-------+         │
 │ | Id | User | Host      | db   | Command | Time | State |        │
 │ +----+------+-----------+------+---------+------+-------+         │
 │ |  1 | root | localhost | NULL | Query   |    0 | NULL  |        │
 │ +----+------+-----------+------+---------+------+-------+         │
 │ 1 row in set (0.01 sec)                                          │
 │                                                                  │
 │ Query OK, 0 rows affected (0.00 sec)                            │
 │                                                                  │
 │ +---------------------------------------------------------        │
 │ | Grants for monty@localhost                                     │
 │ +---------------------------------------------------------        │
 │ | GRANT ALL PRIVILEGES ON *.* TO 'monty'@'localhost'            │
 │ | IDENTIFIED BY PASSWORD '*BF06A06D69EC935E85659FCDED1F6A80     │
 │ | WITH GRANT OPTION                                         ┌─┐  │
 │ +------------------------------------------------------     └─┘  │
 │ 1 row in set (0.00 sec)                                     ▼    │
 └──────────────────────────────────────────────────────────────────┘
```

*MySQL automatically stores user passwords in encrypted form.*

```
 ┌──────────────────────────────────────────────────────────────────┐
 │ ⊛  Linux - Shell - Konsole                        ▽ ▢ ⊗           │
 ├──────────────────────────────────────────────────────────────────┤
 │ Session  Edit  View  Bookmarks  Settings  Help                   │
 ├──────────────────────────────────────────────────────────────────┤
 │ user> mysql -u monty -p                                    ▲     │
 │ Enter password:                                                  │
 │ Welcome to the MySQL monitor.  Commands end with ; or \g.        │
 │ Your MySQL connection id is 6 to server version: 4.1.10-st       │
 │                                                                  │
 │ Type 'help;' or '\h' for help. Type '\c' to clear the buff       │
 │                                                                  │
 │ mysql> SELECT USER();                                            │
 │ +-----------------+                                              │
 │ | USER()          |                                              │
 │ +-----------------+                                              │
 │ | monty@localhost |                                              │
 │ +-----------------+                                              │
 │ 1 row in set (0.00 sec)                                          │
 │                                                                  │
 │ mysql> █                                                    ▼    │
 └──────────────────────────────────────────────────────────────────┘
```

*The password has in fact been typed after the "Enter password:" prompt but it does not appear as text in the window for security purposes.*

# Summary

- A function is an SQL keyword, followed by parentheses, that performs a specific operation when it is called

- Data can be specified as arguments within function parentheses

- SQL function names and syntax vary from one DBMS to another

- A section of a text string can be extracted with the SUBSTRING() function

- Strings can be converted to uppercase with the UPPER() function or to lowercase with the LOWER() function

- The SOUNDEX() function will return data that matches, or is similar to, a specified string

- The MOD() function is useful to determine odd or even values

- Floating-point values can be rounded up to the nearest integer with the CEILING() function or down with the FLOOR() function

- The RAND() function returns a random number from 0 to 1.0

- Individual components of a DATE data type can be returned by the DAYOFMONTH(), MONTHNAME() and YEAR() functions

- Individual components of a TIME data type can be returned with the SECOND(), MINUTE() and HOUR() functions

- The current date is returned by the CURDATE() function and the current time is returned by the CURTIME() function

- A combined DATETIME is returned by the NOW() function

- Threads can be seen with a SHOW PROCESSLIST statement and individual threads can be terminated with the KILL() function

- The GRANT statement is used to create new users by specifying their name, privileges and password

- A user's privileges level can be examined with a SHOW GRANTS statement

# Grouping table data

This chapter introduces SQL "aggregate" functions which are used to summarize table data values. It also explains how data can usefully be grouped and how those groups can be filtered.

## Covers

## Chapter Eleven

# Finding summary values

SQL aggregate functions operate on multiple rows of a database table to perform a pre-ordained calculation and then return a single value. The returned value is a summary of data within that column rather than an actual item of data.

*Any rows of the column that contain a NULL value are totally ignored by the AVG() function.*

The AVG() aggregate function returns a summarized average value of all the values within the column specified as its argument. It counts both the number of rows and the sum of their values, then divides the total value by the total number of rows.

The MAX() aggregate function returns the single highest value in the column specified as its argument. It compares the value on the first row to that on the second row and discards the lower value. It then compares the retained value to that on the next row and again discards the lower value. The operation continues in this manner until the value on the final row has been compared – when the remaining retained value is the highest in that column. Similarly, the MIN() aggregate function returns the single lowest value in a column by discarding the higher value in each comparison.

In the following SQL script example the average, maximum and minimum values are calculated for the "price" column.

*avg-max-min.sql*
*(part of)*

```
# use the "my_database" database
USE my_database;

# create a table called "multimeters"
CREATE TABLE IF NOT EXISTS multimeters
(
  id       INT            AUTO_INCREMENT PRIMARY KEY,
  model    CHAR(10)       NOT NULL,
  price    DECIMAL(3,2)   NOT NULL
);

# insert 3 records into the "multimeters" table
INSERT INTO multimeters (model, price)
  VALUES ("Standard", 11.75);
INSERT INTO multimeters (model, price)
  VALUES ("Super", 19.50);
INSERT INTO multimeters (model, price)
  VALUES ("DeLuxe", 24.99);
```

*avg-max-min.sql*
*(cont'd)*

```sql
# display all data in the "multimeters" table
SELECT * FROM multimeters;

# get the average price
SELECT AVG(price) AS avg_price
FROM multimeters;

# get the maximum price and minimum price
SELECT MAX(price) AS max_price, MIN(price) AS min_price
FROM multimeters;

# delete this sample table
DROP TABLE IF EXISTS multimeters;
```

*Notice here how multiple aggregate function calls are made from a single SELECT statement.*

*Some DBMS', including MySQL, allow the MIN() and MAX() functions to be used on text values – MAX() returns the value that would be last if the values in that column were sorted alphabetically and MIN() returns the value that would be first if the values in that column were sorted alphabetically.*

```
MySQL Command Line Client                    _ □ ×

mysql> source C:\SQL\avg-max-min.sql
Database changed
Query OK, 0 rows affected (0.64 sec)

Query OK, 1 row affected (0.07 sec)

Query OK, 1 row affected (0.03 sec)

Query OK, 1 row affected (0.02 sec)

+----+----------+--------+
| id | model    | price  |
+----+----------+--------+
|  1 | Standard | 11.75  |
|  2 | Super    | 19.50  |
|  3 | DeLuxe   | 24.99  |
+----+----------+--------+
3 rows in set (0.03 sec)

+-----------+
| avg_price |
+-----------+
| 18.746667 |
+-----------+
1 row in set (0.00 sec)

+-----------+-----------+
| max_price | min_price |
+-----------+-----------+
|     24.99 |     11.75 |
+-----------+-----------+
1 row in set (0.03 sec)

Query OK, 0 rows affected (0.13 sec)

mysql> _
```

# Counting rows

The COUNT() aggregate function can determine the total number of rows in a database table. It can also count the number of rows in a specific column that do not contain a NULL value.

To return the total number of rows that a table contains the ★ wildcard character must be specified as the function's argument:

```
COUNT ( * )
```

To return the number of non-empty rows in a particular column the column's name must be specified as the function's argument:

```
COUNT ( column-name )
```

The SQL script example below creates a table populated with five records. Only two records have non-NULL values in the "email" column. The first call to the COUNT() function returns the total number of rows in this table. The second call to the COUNT() function returns just the number of rows where the "email" column does not contain a NULL value.

*count.sql*
*(part of)*

```
# use the "my_database" database
USE my_database;

# create a table called "members"
CREATE TABLE IF NOT EXISTS members
(
   id       INT    AUTO_INCREMENT       PRIMARY KEY,
   name     CHAR(10)      NOT NULL,
   email    VARCHAR(30)
);

# insert 5 records into the "members" table
INSERT INTO members (name)
   VALUES ("Abraham");

INSERT INTO members (name, email)
   VALUES ("Homer", "homer@mailserver.usa");
```

*count.sql*
*(cont'd)*

```
INSERT INTO members (name)
  VALUES ("Marge");

INSERT INTO members (name, email)
  VALUES("Bart", "bart@mailserver.usa");

INSERT INTO members (name) VALUES ("Lisa");

# count the total number of rows
SELECT COUNT(*) AS total_number_of_rows
FROM members;

# count the total number of rows
SELECT COUNT(email) AS rows_with_email_addresses
FROM members;

# delete this sample table
DROP TABLE IF EXISTS members;
```

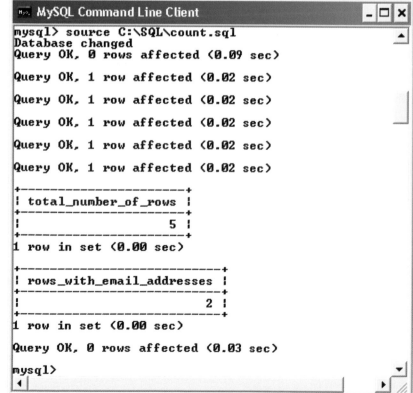

*Specifying the * wildcard character as the COUNT() argument returns the total number of rows including those containing NULL values – columns with NULL values are ignored, however, when a column name is specified as the COUNT() argument.*

# Discovering total values

The SUM() aggregate function returns the sum total of all values in the column specified as its argument. It can return the total of specific rows if the SELECT statement is qualified by a WHERE clause. It can also return the total of a calculated value by including an arithmetical expression within its parentheses.

In the following SQL script example, a table is populated with five records that contain order numbers and unit cost values. The first call to the SUM() function performs an addition that returns the total cost of all values from order number "10031". The second call to the SUM() function performs a multiplication that returns the total cost of values from order number "10030".

*sum.sql*
*(part of)*

```
# use the "my_database" database
USE my_database;

# create a table called "star_orders"
CREATE TABLE IF NOT EXISTS star_orders
(
  id         INT      AUTO_INCREMENT      PRIMARY KEY,
  order_num  INT               NOT NULL,
  cost_each  DECIMAL(6,2)  NOT NULL,
  quantity   INT               DEFAULT 1
);

# insert 5 records into the "star_orders" table
INSERT INTO star_orders (order_num,cost_each,quantity)
  VALUES (10030, 217.50, 2);
INSERT INTO star_orders (order_num, cost_each)
  VALUES (10031, 72.50);
INSERT INTO star_orders (order_num, cost_each)
  VALUES (10032, 299.75);
INSERT INTO star_orders (order_num, cost_each)
  VALUES (10031, 29.25);
INSERT INTO star_orders (order_num, cost_each)
  VALUES (10031, 148.25);

# display all data in the "star_orders" table
SELECT * FROM star_orders;
```

*Columns that contain a NULL value are ignored by the SUM() function.*

*sum.sql*
*(cont'd)*

```
# get total cost for order number 10031
SELECT SUM(cost_each) AS total_for_order_10031
FROM star_orders WHERE order_num = 10031;

# get total cost for order number 10030
SELECT SUM(cost_each*quantity) AS total_for_order_10030
FROM star_orders WHERE order_num = 10030;

# delete this sample table
DROP TABLE IF EXISTS star_orders;
```

*All the SQL aggregate functions – SUM(), COUNT(), AVG(), MAX() and MIN() – can perform calculations on multiple column values, like the second call to the SUM() function in this example.*

```
MySQL Command Line Client                                    _ □ ×

mysql> source C:\SQL\sum.sql
Database changed
Query OK, 0 rows affected (0.13 sec)

Query OK, 1 row affected (0.02 sec)

Query OK, 1 row affected (0.02 sec)

Query OK, 1 row affected (0.02 sec)

Query OK, 1 row affected (0.03 sec)

Query OK, 1 row affected (0.02 sec)

+----+-----------+-----------+----------+
| id | order_num | cost_each | quantity |
+----+-----------+-----------+----------+
|  1 |     10030 |    217.50 |        2 |
|  2 |     10031 |     72.50 |        1 |
|  3 |     10032 |    299.75 |        1 |
|  4 |     10031 |     29.25 |        1 |
|  5 |     10031 |    148.25 |        1 |
+----+-----------+-----------+----------+
5 rows in set (0.00 sec)

+-----------------------+
| total_for_order_10031 |
+-----------------------+
|                250.00 |
+-----------------------+
1 row in set (0.00 sec)

+-----------------------+
| total_for_order_10030 |
+-----------------------+
|                435.00 |
+-----------------------+
1 row in set (0.00 sec)

Query OK, 0 rows affected (0.03 sec)
```

# Working with distinct values

The COUNT() aggregate function can be forced to ignore a row that contains a value duplicating a value which has already appeared in a previously counted row. This is achieved by adding the DISTINCT keyword before the specified column name within the COUNT() function's parentheses.

Using the DISTINCT keyword ensures the COUNT() function will only count rows with unique values in the specified column.

The DISTINCT keyword can also be used to retrieve only unique text values from a column.

The example below demonstrates the effect on counting rows in a table both with and without the DISTINCT keyword. It also lists all the unique values from the "stone" column.

*distinct.sql*
*(part of)*

```
# use the "my_database" database
USE my_database;

# create a table called "rings"
CREATE TABLE IF NOT EXISTS rings
(
    id        INT          AUTO_INCREMENT PRIMARY KEY,
    stone     CHAR(10)     NOT NULL,
    price     DECIMAL(3,2) NOT NULL
);

# insert 5 records into the "rings" table
INSERT INTO rings (stone,price) VALUES ("Ruby", 40.00);
INSERT INTO rings (stone,price) VALUES("Emerald",40.00);
INSERT INTO rings (stone,price) VALUES("Diamond",60.00);
INSERT INTO rings (stone,price) VALUES("Diamond",50.00);
INSERT INTO rings (stone,price) VALUES("Garnet", 40.00);

# display all data in the "rings" table
SELECT * FROM rings;

# get the total number of rows
SELECT COUNT(price) AS num_prices FROM rings;

# get the number of unique rows
SELECT COUNT(DISTINCT price) AS num_distinct_prices
FROM rings;
```

*The DISTINCT keyword cannot be used with the * wildcard character in the COUNT() function – a column name must be specified.*

*distinct.sql*
*(cont'd)*

```
# get all the unique stone values
SELECT DISTINCT stone AS unique_stone_names FROM rings;

# delete this sample table
DROP TABLE IF EXISTS rings;
```

*Some DBMS'
allow the
DISTINCT keyword
to be used with
other aggregate
functions, such as SUM().*

```
 MySQL Command Line Client                    _ □ ✕

mysql> source C:\SQL\distinct.sql
Database changed
Query OK, 0 rows affected (0.07 sec)

Query OK, 1 row affected (0.02 sec)

Query OK, 1 row affected (0.02 sec)

Query OK, 1 row affected (0.04 sec)

Query OK, 1 row affected (0.03 sec)

Query OK, 1 row affected (0.03 sec)

+----+----------+--------+
| id | stone    | price  |
+----+----------+--------+
|  1 | Ruby     | 40.00  |
|  2 | Emerald  | 40.00  |
|  3 | Diamond  | 60.00  |
|  4 | Diamond  | 50.00  |
|  5 | Garnet   | 40.00  |
+----+----------+--------+
5 rows in set (0.00 sec)

+------------+
| num_prices |
+------------+
|          5 |
+------------+
1 row in set (0.00 sec)

+---------------------+
| num_distinct_prices |
+---------------------+
|                   3 |
+---------------------+
1 row in set (0.01 sec)

+--------------------+
| unique_stone_names |
+--------------------+
| Ruby               |
| Emerald            |
| Diamond            |
| Garnet             |
+--------------------+
4 rows in set (0.00 sec)

Query OK, 0 rows affected (0.01 sec)
```

# Creating data groups

All previous examples in this chapter have used aggregate functions to perform a single operation on all the data in a column, or on data that matches a specified WHERE clause. This process can be refined by first arranging the data into logical groups so that the aggregate function operation can be performed on each group.

Data can be grouped by adding a GROUP BY clause to the end of a SELECT statement. This specifies a column name around which to arrange the groups. An aggregate function will then operate once on each group.

In this example the data is first grouped around the "wood" column – the COUNT() function operates on each group to return the number of items in each type of wood. Next the data is grouped around the "item" column – the COUNT() function returns the number of woods for each type of item.

*by-group.sql*
*(part of)*

```
# use the "my_database" database
USE my_database;

# create a table called "cabinets"
CREATE TABLE IF NOT EXISTS cabinets
(
    id       INT    AUTO_INCREMENT      PRIMARY KEY,
    wood     CHAR(10)     NOT NULL,
    item     CHAR(20)     NOT NULL
);

# insert 5 records into the "cabinets" table
INSERT INTO cabinets (wood, item)
  VALUES ("Pine", "Bookcase");
INSERT INTO cabinets (wood, item)
  VALUES ("Beech", "Bookcase");
INSERT INTO cabinets (wood, item)
  VALUES ("Oak", "Bookcase");
INSERT INTO cabinets (wood, item)
  VALUES ("Pine", "Display Case");
INSERT INTO cabinets (wood, item)
  VALUES ("Oak", "Display Case");

# display all data in the "cabinets" table
SELECT * FROM cabinets;
```

*by-group.sql*
*(cont'd)*

```
# get the number of items for each type of wood
SELECT wood, COUNT(*) AS num_items
FROM cabinets GROUP BY wood;

# get the number of woods for each type of item
SELECT item, COUNT(*) AS num_woods
FROM cabinets GROUP BY item;

# delete this sample table
DROP TABLE IF EXISTS cabinets;
```

*A GROUP BY clause must appear in the SELECT statement after any WHERE clause and before ORDER BY clause.*

```
MySQL Command Line Client                        _ □ ×

mysql> source C:\SQL\by-group.sql
Database changed
Query OK, 0 rows affected (0.10 sec)

Query OK, 1 row affected (0.01 sec)

Query OK, 1 row affected (0.03 sec)

Query OK, 1 row affected (0.01 sec)

Query OK, 1 row affected (0.02 sec)

Query OK, 1 row affected (0.02 sec)

+----+-------+--------------+
| id | wood  | item         |
+----+-------+--------------+
|  1 | Pine  | Bookcase     |
|  2 | Beech | Bookcase     |
|  3 | Oak   | Bookcase     |
|  4 | Pine  | Display Case |
|  5 | Oak   | Display Case |
+----+-------+--------------+
5 rows in set (0.00 sec)

+-------+-----------+
| wood  | num_items |
+-------+-----------+
| Beech |         1 |
| Oak   |         2 |
| Pine  |         2 |
+-------+-----------+
3 rows in set (0.03 sec)

+--------------+-----------+
| item         | num_woods |
+--------------+-----------+
| Bookcase     |         3 |
| Display Case |         2 |
+--------------+-----------+
2 rows in set (0.00 sec)
```

# Filtering grouped data

Specific groups can be selected for inclusion in a SELECT statement in a similar way that specific rows can be selected using a WHERE clause. The WHERE clause works on rows of data but cannot be used to filter groups of data. Instead, the HAVING keyword is used to filter groups.

A HAVING clause is very similar to a WHERE clause – except that WHERE filters rows and HAVING filters groups.

Another distinction to make between these two clauses is that the WHERE clause filters before data is grouped and the HAVING clause filters after data is grouped.

The following SQL script example filters out all items priced below 150.00 with a WHERE clause – this leaves 1 item each in the "Red" group and "Terracotta" group, and 2 items in the "Blue" group. It then filters out groups that contain just a single item with a HAVING clause – leaving just the "Blue" group.

*having.sql*
*(part of)*

```
# use the "my_database" database
USE my_database;

# create a table called "sofabeds"
CREATE TABLE IF NOT EXISTS sofabeds
(
    id        INT       AUTO_INCREMENT      PRIMARY KEY,
    name      CHAR(10)        NOT NULL,
    color     CHAR(10)        NOT NULL,
    price     DECIMAL(6,2)  NOT NULL
);

# insert 5 records into the "sofabeds" table
INSERT INTO sofabeds (name, color, price)
    VALUES ("Milan", "Blue", 199.99);
INSERT INTO sofabeds (name, color, price)
    VALUES ("Firenze", "Red", 144.99);
INSERT INTO sofabeds (name, color, price)
    VALUES ("Vivaldi", "Terracotta", 199.99);
INSERT INTO sofabeds (name, color, price)
    VALUES ("Vienna", "Blue", 164.99);
INSERT INTO sofabeds (name, color, price)
    VALUES ("Roma", "Red", 249.99);
```

*having.sql*
*(cont'd)*

```
# display all data in the "sofabeds" table
SELECT * FROM sofabeds;

# get the number of items for each color
# where the price exceeds 150.00 and
# when there is more than 1 item for that color
SELECT color, COUNT(*) AS num_items_over_150
FROM sofabeds
WHERE price >= 150.00
GROUP BY color
HAVING COUNT(*) > 1;

# delete this sample table
DROP TABLE IF EXISTS sofabeds;
```

*Only use a HAVING clause after a GROUP BY clause – use a WHERE clause to filter rows.*

```
MySQL Command Line Client                    _ □ ✕

mysql> source C:\SQL\having.sql
Database changed
Query OK, 0 rows affected (0.10 sec)

Query OK, 1 row affected (0.04 sec)

Query OK, 1 row affected (0.01 sec)

Query OK, 1 row affected (0.03 sec)

Query OK, 1 row affected (0.02 sec)

Query OK, 1 row affected (0.02 sec)

+----+---------+------------+--------+
| id | name    | color      | price  |
+----+---------+------------+--------+
|  1 | Milan   | Blue       | 199.99 |
|  2 | Firenze | Red        | 144.99 |
|  3 | Vivaldi | Terracotta | 199.99 |
|  4 | Vienna  | Blue       | 164.99 |
|  5 | Roma    | Red        | 249.99 |
+----+---------+------------+--------+
5 rows in set (0.00 sec)

+-------+-------------------+
| color | num_items_over_150 |
+-------+-------------------+
| Blue  |                 2 |
+-------+-------------------+
1 row in set (0.00 sec)

Query OK, 0 rows affected (0.04 sec)

mysql> _
```

# Sorting filtered group data

A GROUP BY clause cannot be relied upon to sort groups into order, but an ORDER BY clause can be added at the very end of a SELECT statement for this purpose.

It is important that multiple clauses in a SELECT statement appear in the correct order. The table below reviews the correct order:

| Clause | Specifies |
| --- | --- |
| SELECT | Column/s or expressions to return |
| FROM | Table to retrieve data from |
| WHERE | Row-level filter |
| GROUP BY | Column to group around |
| HAVING | Group-level filter |
| ORDER BY | Return sort order |

Each one of these clauses appears in the following example, which sorts the returned groups into numerical order.

*sort-group.sql*
*(part of)*

```
# use the "my_database" database
USE my_database;

# create a table called "tub"
CREATE TABLE IF NOT EXISTS tub
(
    id        INT            AUTO_INCREMENT PRIMARY KEY,
    num       INT            NOT NULL,
    ref       VARCHAR(10)    NOT NULL,
    qty       INT            DEFAULT 1,
    col       CHAR(10)       NOT NULL
);

# insert 10 records into the "tub" table
INSERT INTO tub (num,ref,col) VALUES (8004,101,"Red");
INSERT INTO tub (num,ref,col) VALUES (8004,103,"Lime");
INSERT INTO tub (num,ref,col) VALUES (8004,104,"Blue");
INSERT INTO tub (num,ref,col) VALUES (8003,104,"Blue");
INSERT INTO tub (num,ref,col) VALUES (8002,105,"Red");
INSERT INTO tub (num,ref,col) VALUES (8002,102,"Lime");
```

*sort-group.sql*
*(cont'd)*

```sql
INSERT INTO tub (num,ref,col) VALUES (8002,103,"Pink");
INSERT INTO tub (num,ref,col) VALUES (8001,104,"Red");
INSERT INTO tub (num,ref,col) VALUES (8001,105,"Lime");
INSERT INTO tub (num,ref,col) VALUES (8004,102,"Blue");

# display all data in the "tub" table
SELECT * FROM tub;

# get the order number and number of items ordered
# where the color is not Pink
# and the number of items ordered is fewer than 3
# sorted by order number
SELECT num, COUNT(*) AS num_items
FROM tub WHERE col != "Pink"
GROUP BY num HAVING COUNT(*) < 3 ORDER BY num;

# delete this sample table
DROP TABLE IF EXISTS tub;
```

*This example uses a variety of the techniques introduced in this chapter.*

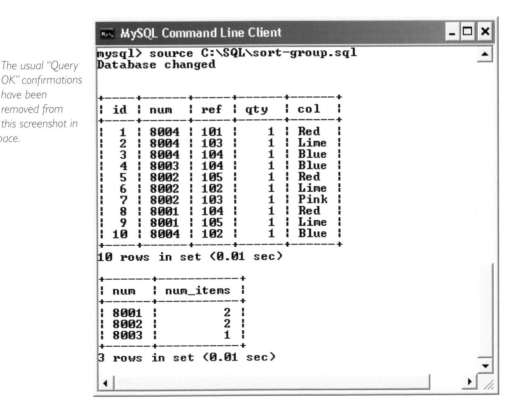

*The usual "Query OK" confirmations have been removed from this screenshot in order to save space.*

# Summary

- Aggregate functions operate on multiple rows of a database table to perform a pre-ordained calculation, then return a single value

- The five standard aggregate functions in SQL are AVG(), MAX(), MIN(), SUM() and COUNT()

- Each aggregate function must state the column/s to operate on as the argument within its parentheses

- The AVG() function returns the average of all the values in its specified column

- MAX() returns the highest value of the data within its specified column and MIN() returns its lowest value

- SUM() returns the sum total of all the values within the specified column

- COUNT() can specify the * wildcard character as its argument in order to return the total number of rows in a table, or a column name to return the number of non-empty rows in that column

- NULL data values are generally ignored by aggregate functions – except when the COUNT() function specifies the * wildcard character as its argument

- The DISTINCT keyword ensures that only unique instances of a data value are operated upon

- Data can be grouped with a GROUP BY clause to allow an aggregate function to operate on each group

- A WHERE clause filters rows before data is grouped and a HAVING clause filters groups after data is grouped

- The GROUP BY clause does not ensure any sort order – an ORDER BY clause must be used to specify a sort order

- The clauses in a SELECT statement must appear in the correct order – SELECT, FROM, WHERE, GROUP BY, HAVING, ORDER BY

# Making complex queries

This chapter introduces some advanced techniques that allow data from multiple tables to be returned by a single query. It also demonstrates how the returns from multiple SELECT queries can be combined as a single "results set".

## Covers

**Chapter Twelve**

# Using sub-queries

Every SELECT statement is an SQL query. Many DBMS' allow a SELECT statement to be nested within another SELECT statement. The inner SELECT statement is known as a sub-query.

Sub-queries are useful to retrieve data from a table specifying what an outer SELECT statement should return from another table. For instance, imagine a table named "customers" containing name and account numbers and another table named "orders" containing order numbers and customer account numbers. A query to identify the name of a customer who placed a particular order might look like this:

```
SELECT name FROM customers WHERE acc_num IN
   ( SELECT acc_num FROM orders WHERE ord_num = 4 );
```

The inner sub-query is processed first. In this case it returns the customer account number for order number 4 in the "orders" table. The outer query then matches the customer account number and returns the name of that customer.

*Sub-queries are not supported in MySQL prior to version 4.1.*

Notice that both tables have a column named "acc_num". This is perfectly acceptable – each column can be referenced explicitly using dot syntax as "customers.acc_num" and "orders.acc_num".

SELECT statements that contain sub-queries can be difficult to read and debug as they become more complex. There is, however, often an alternative to sub-queries. The following SQL script rewrites the example given above to provide the same functionality without using a sub-query.

*subquery.sql*
*(part of)*

```
use the "my_database" database
USE my_database;

# create a table called "customers"
CREATE TABLE IF NOT EXISTS customers
( acc_num INT PRIMARY KEY, name CHAR(20) NOT NULL );

# insert 2 records into the "customers" table
INSERT INTO customers (acc_num, name)
   VALUES (123, "T.Smith");
INSERT INTO customers (acc_num, name)
   VALUES (124, "P.Jones");
```

subquery.sql
(cont'd)

```
# create a table called "orders"
CREATE TABLE IF NOT EXISTS orders
( ord_num INT PRIMARY KEY, acc_num INT NOT NULL );

# insert 2 records into the "orders" table
INSERT INTO orders (ord_num, acc_num) VALUES (3, 123);
INSERT INTO orders (ord_num, acc_num) VALUES (4, 124);

# display all data in "customers" and "orders" tables
SELECT * FROM customers; SELECT * FROM orders;

# retrieve the name of the customer placing order 4
SELECT  ord_num, customers.acc_num, name
FROM customers, orders
WHERE  customers.acc_num = orders.acc_num
AND orders.ord_num = 4;

# delete these sample tables
DROP TABLE IF EXISTS customers;
DROP TABLE IF EXISTS orders;
```

*Always use the dot syntax to explicitly identify table columns wherever there is possible ambiguity.*

*The usual "Query OK" confirmations have been removed from all further screenshots within this book in order to save space.*

```
mysql> source /home/SQL/subquery.sql
Database changed
+---------+---------+
| acc_num | name    |
+---------+---------+
|     123 | T.Smith |
|     124 | P.Jones |
+---------+---------+
2 rows in set (0.00 sec)


+---------+---------+
| ord_num | acc_num |
+---------+---------+
|       3 |     123 |
|       4 |     124 |
+---------+---------+
2 rows in set (0.00 sec)


+---------+---------+---------+
| ord_num | acc_num | name    |
+---------+---------+---------+
|       4 |     124 | P.Jones |
+---------+---------+---------+
1 row in set (0.00 sec)
```

# Sub-query calculated fields

A sub-query can be used to generate a calculated field that returns values from a table to an outer SELECT statement.

Given the "customers" and "orders" tables from the previous example, a sub-query could use the COUNT() aggregate function to calculate how many orders have been placed by each account number in the "orders" table. The outer SELECT statement can then retrieve each customer name to display with this calculated field. The SELECT query and sub-query could look like this:

```
SELECT name,
  ( SELECT COUNT(*) FROM orders
    WHERE orders.acc_num = customers.acc_num )
AS number_of_orders FROM customers
ORDER BY customers.acc_num;
```

The script below produces the same result without a sub-query. Both methods generate a "number_of_orders" calculated field alongside customer names, sorted by their account number.

*subquery-calc.sql*
*(part of)*

```
# use the "my_database" database
USE my_database;

# create a table called "customers"
CREATE TABLE IF NOT EXISTS customers
( acc_num INT PRIMARY KEY, name CHAR(20) NOT NULL );

# insert 3 records into the "customers" table
INSERT INTO customers (acc_num, name)
  VALUES (123, "T.Smith");
INSERT INTO customers (acc_num, name)
  VALUES (124, "P.Jones");
INSERT INTO customers (acc_num, name)
  VALUES (125, "H.Nicks");

# create a table called "orders"
CREATE TABLE IF NOT EXISTS orders
( ord_num INT PRIMARY KEY, acc_num INT NOT NULL );

# insert 5 records into the "orders" table
INSERT INTO orders (ord_num, acc_num) VALUES (1, 123);
INSERT INTO orders (ord_num, acc_num) VALUES (2, 124);
```

subquery-calc.sql
(cont'd)

```
INSERT INTO orders (ord_num, acc_num) VALUES (3, 125);
INSERT INTO orders (ord_num, acc_num) VALUES (4, 125);
INSERT INTO orders (ord_num, acc_num) VALUES (5, 123);

# display all data in "customers" and "orders" tables
SELECT * FROM customers; SELECT * FROM orders;

# get the number of orders per customer
SELECT name, COUNT(*) AS number_of_orders
FROM   customers, orders
WHERE customers.acc_num = orders.acc_num
GROUP BY name ORDER BY customers.acc_num;

# delete these sample tables
DROP TABLE IF EXISTS customers;
DROP TABLE IF EXISTS orders;
```

```
╭──────────────────────────────────────────────────────────╮
│  ▣  Linux - Shell - Konsole          ▽ □ ✕               │
├──────────────────────────────────────────────────────────┤
│ Session  Edit  View  Bookmarks  Settings  Help           │
├──────────────────────────────────────────────────────────┤
│ mysql> source /home/SQL/subquery-calc.sql                │
│ Database changed                                         │
│ +---------+---------+                                    │
│ | acc_num | name    |                                    │
│ +---------+---------+                                    │
│ |     123 | T.Smith |                                    │
│ |     124 | P.Jones |                                    │
│ |     125 | H.Nicks |                                    │
│ +---------+---------+                                    │
│ 3 rows in set (0.00 sec)                                 │
│                                                          │
│ +---------+---------+                                    │
│ | ord_num | acc_num |                                    │
│ +---------+---------+                                    │
│ |       1 |     123 |                                    │
│ |       2 |     124 |                                    │
│ |       3 |     125 |                                    │
│ |       4 |     125 |                                    │
│ |       5 |     123 |                                    │
│ +---------+---------+                                    │
│ 5 rows in set (0.00 sec)                                 │
│ +---------+---------+------------------+                 │
│ | name    | acc_num | number_of_orders |                │
│ +---------+---------+------------------+                 │
│ | T.Smith |     123 |                2 |                │
│ | P.Jones |     124 |                1 |                │
│ | H.Nicks |     125 |                2 |                │
│ +---------+---------+------------------+                 │
│ 3 rows in set (0.03 sec)                                 │
╰──────────────────────────────────────────────────────────╯
```

# Combining queries

Multiple SELECT queries can be made to combine their returns into a single "result set" using the UNION keyword. The SELECT statements may query the same table, or different tables, but each statement must have the same format:

- Each query must specify the same column names, expressions and aggregate function calls

- Specified column names, expressions and function calls must appear in precisely the same order in each query

- Column data types must be compatible – they need not be identical, but of similar types that can be converted. For instance, similar numeric types or similar date types

There are no standard limits to the number of SELECT queries that can be combined with the UNION keyword. The following example combines the returns from three SELECT queries, made to three different tables, into a single common result set.

*union.sql*
*(part of)*

```
# use the "my_database" database
USE my_database;

# create a table called "ps_games"
CREATE TABLE IF NOT EXISTS ps_games
( code VARCHAR(10), title CHAR(20), ages VARCHAR(3) );

# insert 2 records into the "ps_games" table
INSERT INTO ps_games (code, title, ages)
  VALUES ("567/3573", "Crash Bash Platinum", "3+");
INSERT INTO ps_games (code, title, ages)
  VALUES ("567/0301", "The Italian Job", "11+");

# create a table called "xbox_games"
CREATE TABLE IF NOT EXISTS xbox_games
( code VARCHAR(10), title CHAR(20), ages VARCHAR(3) );

# insert 2 records into the "xbox_games" table
INSERT INTO xbox_games (code, title, ages)
  VALUES ("567/2660", "Blinx", "3+");
INSERT INTO xbox_games (code, title, ages)
  VALUES ("567/0569", "Turok Evolution", "15+");
```

*Refer to your DBMS documentation to check that it does not impose a maximum statement restriction.*

*union.sql*
*(cont'd)*

```
# create a table called "cube_games"
CREATE TABLE IF NOT EXISTS cube_games
( code VARCHAR(10), title CHAR(20), ages VARCHAR(3) );

# insert 2 records into the "cube_games" table
INSERT INTO cube_games (code, title, ages)
  VALUES ("567/0428", "Scooby-Doo", "3+");
INSERT INTO cube_games (code, title, ages)
  VALUES ("567/0411", "Resident Evil", "15+");

# display all data in "ps_games", "xbox_games"
# and "cube_games" as a single result set
SELECT * FROM ps_games
UNION
SELECT * FROM xbox_games
UNION
SELECT * FROM cube_games;

# delete these sample tables
DROP TABLE IF EXISTS ps_games;
DROP TABLE IF EXISTS xbox_games;
DROP TABLE IF EXISTS cube_games;
```

*The data within the tables is not actually affected – the UNION only determines how the returns are presented.*

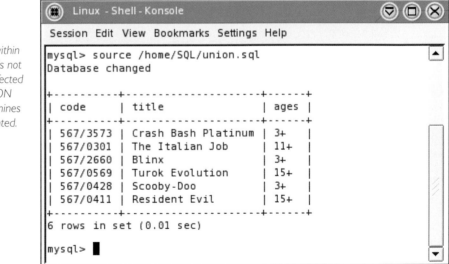

```
mysql> source /home/SQL/union.sql
Database changed

+----------+----------------------+------+
| code     | title                | ages |
+----------+----------------------+------+
| 567/3573 | Crash Bash Platinum  | 3+   |
| 567/0301 | The Italian Job      | 11+  |
| 567/2660 | Blinx                | 3+   |
| 567/0569 | Turok Evolution      | 15+  |
| 567/0428 | Scooby-Doo           | 3+   |
| 567/0411 | Resident Evil        | 15+  |
+----------+----------------------+------+
6 rows in set (0.01 sec)

mysql>
```

# Handling duplicate rows

The default behavior of the UNION keyword automatically excludes any duplicate rows from the data returned by the SELECT statement.

It is sometimes preferable to have the SELECT statement return all rows, including duplicates, by using a UNION ALL clause rather than just the UNION keyword.

In this example the SQL script creates two tables, each populated with two records – the second rows in each table are identical. The SELECT query using the UNION keyword only returns one instance of that data, whereas the SELECT query using the UNION ALL clause returns both instances.

*union-all.sql*
*(part of)*

```
# use the "my_database" database
USE my_database;

# create a table called "ps2_games" & insert 2 records
CREATE TABLE IF NOT EXISTS ps2_games
( title CHAR(20), ages VARCHAR(3) );
INSERT INTO ps2_games ( title, ages)
  VALUES ("Grand Theft Auto 3", "18+");
INSERT INTO ps2_games (title, ages)
  VALUES ("Colin McRae Rally 3", "11+");

# create a table called "xbox_games" & insert 2 records
CREATE TABLE IF NOT EXISTS xbox_games
( title CHAR(20), ages VARCHAR(3) );
INSERT INTO xbox_games (title, ages)
  VALUES ("Splinter Cell", "15+");
INSERT INTO xbox_games (title, ages)
  VALUES ("Colin McRae Rally 3", "11+");

# display all data in the "ps2_games" and "xbox_games"
SELECT * FROM ps2_games;
SELECT * FROM xbox_games;

# display unique data in "ps2_games" and "xbox_games"
SELECT * FROM ps2_games
UNION
SELECT * FROM xbox_games;
```

*union-all.sql*
*(cont'd)*

```
# display all data in "ps2_games" and "xbox_games"
SELECT * FROM ps2_games
UNION ALL
SELECT * FROM xbox_games;

# delete these sample tables
DROP TABLE IF EXISTS ps2_games;
DROP TABLE IF EXISTS xbox_games;
```

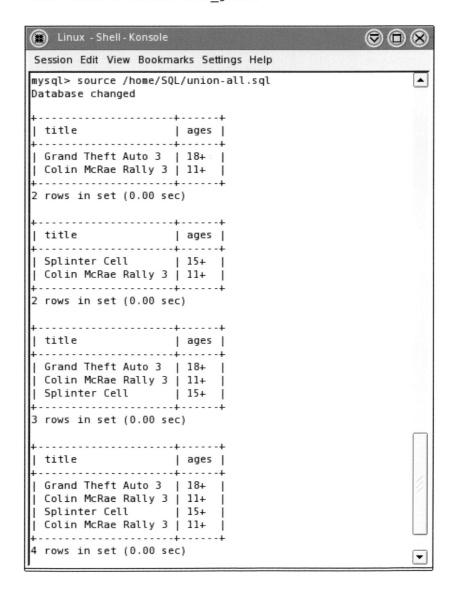

```
mysql> source /home/SQL/union-all.sql
Database changed

+--------------------+------+
| title              | ages |
+--------------------+------+
| Grand Theft Auto 3 | 18+  |
| Colin McRae Rally 3| 11+  |
+--------------------+------+
2 rows in set (0.00 sec)

+--------------------+------+
| title              | ages |
+--------------------+------+
| Splinter Cell      | 15+  |
| Colin McRae Rally 3| 11+  |
+--------------------+------+
2 rows in set (0.00 sec)

+--------------------+------+
| title              | ages |
+--------------------+------+
| Grand Theft Auto 3 | 18+  |
| Colin McRae Rally 3| 11+  |
| Splinter Cell      | 15+  |
+--------------------+------+
3 rows in set (0.00 sec)

+--------------------+------+
| title              | ages |
+--------------------+------+
| Grand Theft Auto 3 | 18+  |
| Colin McRae Rally 3| 11+  |
| Splinter Cell      | 15+  |
| Colin McRae Rally 3| 11+  |
+--------------------+------+
4 rows in set (0.00 sec)
```

# Sorting combined query results

The data returned from multiple tables using the UNION keyword can be sorted into a specified order by adding a single ORDER BY clause after the final SELECT statement. It may appear to apply only to that final SELECT statement, but will, in fact, sort the data returned from all the SELECT statements.

In the following SQL script example, data returned from two tables is combined and sorted into order – first numerically, then alphabetically.

*union-sort.sql*
*(part of)*

```
# use the "my_database" database
USE my_database;

# create a table called "hers" and insert 3 records
CREATE TABLE IF NOT EXISTS hers
( id INT AUTO_INCREMENT PRIMARY KEY, name CHAR(20) );
INSERT INTO hers ( name ) VALUES ("Linda");
INSERT INTO hers ( name ) VALUES ("Donna");
INSERT INTO hers ( name ) VALUES ("Kay");

# create a table called "his" and insert 3 records
CREATE TABLE IF NOT EXISTS his
( id INT AUTO_INCREMENT PRIMARY KEY, name CHAR(20) );
INSERT INTO his ( name ) VALUES ("Michael");
INSERT INTO his ( name ) VALUES ("David");
INSERT INTO his ( name ) VALUES ("Andrew");

# display all data in the "hers" and "his" table
SELECT * FROM hers;
SELECT * FROM his;

# display all data in "hers" and "his"
# sorted by id
SELECT * FROM hers
UNION
SELECT * FROM his ORDER BY id;

# display all data in "hers" and "his"
# sorted by name
SELECT * FROM hers
UNION
SELECT * FROM his ORDER BY name;
```

*union-sort.sql*
*(cont'd)*

```
# delete these sample tables
DROP TABLE IF EXISTS hers;
DROP TABLE IF EXISTS his;
```

```
Linux - Shell - Konsole

Session  Edit  View  Bookmarks  Settings  Help

mysql> source /home/SQL/union-sort.sql
Database changed
+----+--------+
| id | name   |
+----+--------+
|  1 | Linda  |
|  2 | Donna  |
|  3 | Kay    |
+----+--------+
3 rows in set (0.00 sec)

+----+----------+
| id | name     |
+----+----------+
|  1 | Michael  |
|  2 | David    |
|  3 | Andrew   |
+----+----------+
3 rows in set (0.00 sec)

+----+----------+
| id | name     |
+----+----------+
|  1 | Linda    |
|  1 | Michael  |
|  2 | Donna    |
|  2 | David    |
|  3 | Kay      |
|  3 | Andrew   |
+----+----------+
6 rows in set (0.00 sec)

+----+----------+
| id | name     |
+----+----------+
|  3 | Andrew   |
|  2 | David    |
|  2 | Donna    |
|  3 | Kay      |
|  1 | Linda    |
|  1 | Michael  |
+----+----------+
6 rows in set (0.00 sec)
```

# Summary

- A SELECT query nested within another SELECT query is known as a "sub-query"

- An inner SELECT sub-query is always processed before the outer SELECT query in which it is nested

- Sub-queries can retrieve data from a table to specify what an outer SELECT statement should return from another table

- Columns, in tables containing columns with identical names, can be explicitly addressed using dot syntax, as table.column-name

- Like regular SELECT statements, sub-queries can also generate calculated fields

- SELECT statements containing sub-queries can be difficult to read and debug – there is often an alternative way to make the queries

- The data returned from multiple SELECT queries can be combined into a single "result set" using the UNION keyword

- All SELECT queries combined with the UNION keyword must have the same format for their columns and expressions

- Data returned from multiple tables with the UNION keyword automatically excludes any duplicate rows

- The UNION ALL clause ensures that each instance of duplicated rows are included in the returned data

- Data returned from multiple tables using the UNION keyword can be sorted into a specified order by adding a single ORDER BY clause after the final SELECT statement

# Joining database tables

This chapter introduces the important topic of "joins" and explains why they are of such significance in SQL. Examples demonstrate a variety of techniques featuring SELECT queries with joins.

## Covers

**Chapter Thirteen**

# What are joins ?

The ability to dynamically join together multiple tables with a single SELECT query is one of SQL's most powerful features. This allows related data to be efficiently stored in numerous tables, rather than in just one large table.

Storing data in numerous related tables is the essence of relational database design and provides some important benefits. It is necessary to understand relational tables to fully appreciate the significance afforded by the join capability.

For instance, imagine a table containing a product catalog. This could typically have columns for catalog number, product name and product price together with the name and address of the vendor supplying each product. A table of this format containing data on various game products might look like this:

```
+-----------+----------+--------+---------------+----------------------+
| id        | game     | price  | vendor        | location             |
+-----------+----------+--------+---------------+----------------------+
| 371/2209  | Scrabble | 14.50  | Mattel Inc    | El Segundo, CA, USA  |
| 373/2296  | Jenga    |  6.99  | Hasbro Inc    | Pawtucket, RI, USA   |
| 360/9659  | Uno      | 11.99  | Mattel Inc    | El Segundo, CA, USA  |
| 373/5372  | Connect  |  5.99  | J.W.Spear Plc | Enfield, Middx, UK   |
| 370/9470  | Bingo    |  8.99  | J.W.Spear Plc | Enfield, Middx, UK   |
+-----------+----------+--------+---------------+----------------------+
```

Notice how the vendor data is laboriously repeated for catalog items that are created by the same vendor. This is undesirable, especially with a larger catalog, for these main reasons:

- It is an inefficient use of time to repeatedly input the same vendor data for each record

- The database table size requires more space to store the repeated data

- Each instance of the vendor data would need to be individually updated if their information changes – for example, if the vendor relocates to a new address

- There is a possibility that the vendor data might not be input in the exact same format in every record – so creating inconsistent data that may produce misleading returns from SQL queries

It is far more preferable to store the vendor data in a separate table and relate the vendor to the product by an identity reference. In the case of the games products, the previous table data could now appear in two separate tables like this:

*Whenever a table column contains duplicate data consider creating a separate table for that data.*

```
+-----------+---------+----------+---------+
| id        | vendor  | name     | price   |
+-----------+---------+----------+---------+
| 371/2209  |       1 | Scrabble | 14.50   |
| 373/2296  |       2 | Jenga    |  6.99   |
| 360/9659  |       1 | Uno      | 11.99   |
| 373/5372  |       3 | Connect  |  5.99   |
| 370/9470  |       3 | Bingo    |  8.99   |
+-----------+---------+----------+---------+
```

```
+-------+----------------+----------------------+
| id    | name           | location             |
+-------+----------------+----------------------+
|     1 | Mattel Inc     | El Segundo, CA, USA  |
|     2 | Hasbro Inc     | Pawtucket, RI, USA   |
|     3 | J.W.Spear Plc  | Enfield, Middx, UK   |
+-------+----------------+----------------------+
```

These two compact tables store precisely the same information as the previous large table and have these benefits:

- Duplicated vendor data need not be repeatedly entered

- The database tables size requires less space

- A single change is required should the vendor information need to be updated

- The vendor data is assured to be consistent

These tables are both created with the "id" column specified as the **PRIMARY KEY** to ensure that data in that column is unique in each row – so no product code can be duplicated and no vendor information can be duplicated.

Remember that like-named columns can be explicitly addressed using the dot syntax, such as "vendors.id" and "games.id".

The data in both tables can be retrieved using a single SELECT query to join the product data to the associated vendor data.

# Creating a join

The data can be returned from multiple joined tables by stating the table names as a comma-separated listed after the FROM keyword in a SELECT statement.

A WHERE clause <u>must</u> then be added to the SELECT statement to define the relationship between data in each table. This acts as a filter to return only the data that satisfies the specified condition.

The following SQL script example creates the "games" and "vendors" tables shown on page 163. The WHERE clause in a SELECT query defines the relationship between data in the "vendor" column of the "games" table and the "id" column of the "vendors" table.

The SELECT column retrieves specific correctly associated rows from these joined tables, listed under descriptive alias headings.

*join.sql*
*(part of)*

```
# use the "my_database" database
USE my_database;

# create a table called "games"
CREATE TABLE IF NOT EXISTS games
(
    id          VARCHAR(10)    PRIMARY KEY,
    vendor      INT            NOT NULL,
    name        CHAR(20)       NOT NULL,
    price       DECIMAL(6,2)   NOT NULL
);

# insert 5 records into the "games" table
INSERT INTO games (id, vendor, name, price)
    VALUES ("371/2209", 1, "Scrabble", 14.50);
INSERT INTO games (id, vendor, name, price)
    VALUES ("373/2296", 2, "Jenga", 6.99);
INSERT INTO games (id, vendor, name, price)
    VALUES ("360/9659", 1, "Uno", 11.99);
INSERT INTO games (id, vendor, name, price)
    VALUES ("373/5372", 3, "Connect", 5.99);
INSERT INTO games (id, vendor, name, price)
    VALUES ("370/9470", 3, "Bingo", 8.99);
```

*The join does not directly affect the table data itself – it simply extracts the required data dynamically.*

*join.sql
(cont'd)*

```
# create a table called "vendors"
CREATE TABLE IF NOT EXISTS vendors
(
  id         INT              PRIMARY KEY,
  name       CHAR(20)         NOT NULL,
  location   CHAR(20)         NOT NULL
);

# insert 3 records into the "vendors" table
INSERT INTO vendors (id, name, location)
  VALUES (1, "Mattel Inc", "El Segundo, Ca, USA");
INSERT INTO vendors (id, name, location)
  VALUES (2, "Hasbro Inc", "Pawtucket, RI, USA");
INSERT INTO vendors (id, name, location)
  VALUES (3, "J.W.Spear Plc", "Enfield, Middx, UK");
```

*Omission of the WHERE clause will return every row in the first table paired with every row in the second table – 15 rows in this case. This is not the desired result as no association has been made between data in each table.*

```
# display game code, name, price and vendor name
# for each game in the two joined tables
SELECT         games.id      AS ProductCode,
               games.name    AS Game,
               vendors.name  AS Vendor,
               games.price   AS Price
FROM           games, vendors
WHERE          vendors.id = games.vendor;

# delete these sample tables
DROP TABLE games;
DROP TABLE vendors;
```

**MySQL Command Line Client**

```
mysql> source C:\SQL\join.sql
Database changed
+-------------+----------+---------------+--------+
| ProductCode | Game     | Vendor        | Price  |
+-------------+----------+---------------+--------+
| 360/9659    | Uno      | Mattel Inc    | 11.99  |
| 371/2209    | Scrabble | Mattel Inc    | 14.50  |
| 373/2296    | Jenga    | Hasbro Inc    |  6.99  |
| 370/9470    | Bingo    | J.W.Spear Plc |  8.99  |
| 373/5372    | Connect  | J.W.Spear Plc |  5.99  |
+-------------+----------+---------------+--------+
5 rows in set (0.00 sec)
```

# Joining multiple tables

There is theoretically no limit to the number of tables that can be joined by a single SELECT statement. However, the length of time taken to process the query will increase in proportion to the number of tables joined, and their sizes.

When joining multiple tables, the relationship between data in the first two tables must be defined in a WHERE clause, as with the previous example. The relationship of subsequent tables can then be defined using the AND keyword.

This example first defines the relationship between the "vendors" table and the "items" table, then that between the "items" table and the "orders" table. This allows data for a specific order to be retrieved with correctly associated item and vendor information.

*multi-join.sql*
*(part of)*

*Some DBMS' impose their own limit on the number of tables that may be joined by a SELECT statement – check the documentation of your own DBMS for further details.*

```sql
# use the "my_database" database
USE my_database;

# create a table called "items" with 3 records
CREATE TABLE IF NOT EXISTS items
(
    id          INT             PRIMARY KEY,
    vendor      INT             NOT NULL,
    name        CHAR(20)        NOT NULL,
    price       DECIMAL(6,2)    NOT NULL
);

INSERT INTO items (id, vendor, name, price)
    VALUES (601, 2, "Elephants", 147.50);
INSERT INTO items (id, vendor, name, price)
    VALUES (602, 2, "Reindeer",  123.00);
INSERT INTO items (id, vendor, name, price)
    VALUES (603, 1, "Alligators", 185.00);

# create a table called "vendors" with 2 records
CREATE TABLE IF NOT EXISTS vendors
(
    id          INT             PRIMARY KEY,
    name        CHAR(20)        NOT NULL
);
INSERT INTO vendors (id, name) VALUES (1, "Alpha Inc");
INSERT INTO vendors (id, name) VALUES (2, "Zeta Inc");
```

*multi-join.sql*
*(cont'd)*

```
# create a table called "orders" with 3 records
CREATE TABLE IF NOT EXISTS orders
(
  num       INT     PRIMARY KEY,
  item      INT     NOT NULL,
  qty       INT     NOT NULL
);
INSERT INTO orders (num, item, qty)
  VALUES (2805, 603, 10);
INSERT INTO orders (num, item, qty)
  VALUES (2806, 603, 5);
INSERT INTO orders (num, item, qty)
  VALUES (2807, 601, 10);

# display order number, quantity, item name, vendor
# and total order value of order number 2805
SELECT          orders.num              AS Number,
                orders.qty              AS Qty,
                items.name              AS Toy,
                vendors.name            AS Vendor,
                items.price * orders.qty   AS Total
FROM            items, vendors, orders
WHERE           vendors.id = items.vendor
AND             items.id = orders.item
AND             orders.num = 2805;

# delete these sample tables
DROP TABLE IF EXISTS items;
DROP TABLE IF EXISTS vendors;
DROP TABLE IF EXISTS orders;
```

*This SELECT statement specifies an alias name for each of the columns it queries with the AS keyword – some DBMS', such as Oracle, do not require the AS keyword before the alias name.*

```
MySQL Command Line Client                    _ □ ✕

mysql> source C:\SQL\multi-join.sql
Database changed

+--------+-----+-----------+-----------+---------+
| Number | Qty | Toy       | Vendor    | Total   |
+--------+-----+-----------+-----------+---------+
|   2805 |  10 | Alligators | Alpha Inc | 1850.00 |
+--------+-----+-----------+-----------+---------+
1 row in set (0.01 sec)
```

# Creating self joins

The table joins demonstrated in the previous examples in this chapter are known as "equijoins" because the relationship between the tables is defined by a test of equality. This type of join is also referred to as an "inner" join.

The rest of this chapter examines three other types of join – the "self join", the "natural join" and the "outer join".

A self join enables a SELECT query to make more than one reference to the same table. In order to avoid ambiguity it must specify different alias names for the table using the AS keyword in the FROM clause. It can then explicitly address columns from each table using dot syntax.

*In many DBMS' self joins are processed faster than sub-queries.*

The usefulness of a self join may not be immediately apparent without a practical example. Imagine a table containing personnel data, listing the name of each individual and the department where they are employed. A SELECT query could use a self join to return the name of all personnel in the department of any specified individual.

This example stores the personnel data in a table called "staff". In the SELECT statement this table is given two alias names of "s1" and "s2". Consider these to be two virtual tables containing identical data in identical columns.

The WHERE clause explicitly compares column data in the first virtual table with that in the second virtual table to discover the department in which the specified individual is employed. It then returns the name and department for all staff members in that department.

*self-join.sql
(part of)*

```
# use the "my_database" database
USE my_database;

# create a table called "staff"
CREATE TABLE IF NOT EXISTS staff
( dept CHAR(20) NOT NULL, name CHAR(20) PRIMARY KEY );

# insert 6 records into the "staff" table
INSERT INTO staff (dept, name)
  VALUES ("Sales", "Jo Brown");
```

self-join.sql
(cont'd)

```sql
INSERT INTO staff (dept, name)
  VALUES ("Legal", "Max Tiler");
INSERT INTO staff (dept, name)
  VALUES ("Works", "Ed Frost");
INSERT INTO staff (dept, name)
  VALUES ("Sales", "Sue Ebner");
INSERT INTO staff (dept, name)
  VALUES ("Works", "Al Morris");
INSERT INTO staff (dept, name)
  VALUES ("Sales", "Tony West");

# display all data in the "staff" table
SELECT * FROM staff;

# display the all members of staff
# in the same department as Tony West
SELECT   s1.dept AS Department, s1.name AS Name
FROM     staff AS s1, staff AS s2
WHERE    s1.dept = s2.dept AND s2.name = "Tony West";

# delete this sample table
DROP TABLE IF EXISTS staff;
```

Notice that explicit addressing appears in the first part of this SELECT statement – even before the alias names have been specified in the WHERE clause. Always use explicit addressing with self joins to avoid ambiguity.

```
MySQL Command Line Client                          _  □  ✕

mysql> source C:\SQL\self-join.sql
Database changed
+--------+-----------+
| dept   | name      |
+--------+-----------+
| Works  | Al Morris |
| Works  | Ed Frost  |
| Sales  | Jo Brown  |
| Legal  | Max Tiler |
| Sales  | Sue Ebner |
| Sales  | Tony West |
+--------+-----------+
6 rows in set (0.00 sec)
+------------+-----------+
| Department | Name      |
+------------+-----------+
| Sales      | Jo Brown  |
| Sales      | Sue Ebner |
| Sales      | Tony West |
+------------+-----------+
3 rows in set (0.00 sec)

Query OK, 0 rows affected (0.02 sec)
```

# Creating natural joins

All table joins have at least one column that will also appear in another table – allowing the relationship between those tables to be defined. A natural join is simply a technique to eliminate a column that contains duplicate data.

Typically the "★" wildcard character is used to return all the columns from the first table. Then specific, non-duplicating columns are joined from other tables. This is not a radical departure from previous examples, but merely offers alternative syntax rather than specifying each required column individually.

The following SQL script example creates and populates two database tables. Each table contains a column listing common part numbers that can be used to define the relationship between these two tables.

The SELECT query creates aliases for both tables. It then returns all the columns from the "parts" table, using the "p" alias with the "★" wildcard character, and the "price" column from the "parts_prices" table, using the "pp" alias with dot syntax.

natural-join.sql
(part of)

```
# use the "my_database" database
USE my_database;

# create a table called "parts"
CREATE TABLE IF NOT EXISTS parts
( num INT PRIMARY KEY, name CHAR(20)   NOT NULL );

# insert 3 records into the "parts" table
INSERT INTO parts (num, name)
  VALUES (382131, "Standard bracket");
INSERT INTO parts (num, name)
  VALUES (382132, "Slide bracket");
INSERT INTO parts (num, name)
  VALUES (382133, "Low-mount bracket");

# create a table called "parts_prices"
CREATE TABLE IF NOT EXISTS parts_prices
(
  num        INT         PRIMARY KEY,
  price      DECIMAL(6,2) NOT NULL
);
```

*natural-join.sql*
*(cont'd)*

```
# insert 3 records into the "parts_prices" table
INSERT INTO parts_prices (num, price)
  VALUES (382131, 8.99);
INSERT INTO parts_prices (num, price)
  VALUES (382132, 10.99);
INSERT INTO parts_prices (num, price)
  VALUES (382133, 29.99);

# display all data in "parts" and "parts_prices" tables
SELECT * FROM parts; SELECT * FROM parts_prices;

# display each part number, name and price
SELECT        p.*, pp.price
FROM          parts AS p, parts_prices AS pp
WHERE         p.num = pp.num;

# delete these sample tables
DROP TABLE IF EXISTS parts;
DROP TABLE IF EXISTS parts_prices;
```

*Table aliases are useful to shorten the SQL code – especially in more complex SELECT statements.*

```
MySQL Command Line Client                        _ □ ✕

mysql> source C:\SQL\natural-join.sql
Database changed
+--------+---------------------+
| num    | name                |
+--------+---------------------+
| 382131 | Standard bracket    |
| 382132 | Slide bracket       |
| 382133 | Low-mount bracket   |
+--------+---------------------+
3 rows in set (0.00 sec)

+--------+--------+
| num    | price  |
+--------+--------+
| 382131 |   8.99 |
| 382132 |  10.99 |
| 382133 |  29.99 |
+--------+--------+
3 rows in set (0.00 sec)

+--------+---------------------+--------+
| num    | name                | price  |
+--------+---------------------+--------+
| 382131 | Standard bracket    |   8.99 |
| 382132 | Slide bracket       |  10.99 |
| 382133 | Low-mount bracket   |  29.99 |
+--------+---------------------+--------+
3 rows in set (0.00 sec)
```

# Creating outer joins

Mostly table joins will be the standard inner, equijoin type that returns the data from rows where the column data matches for the defined relationship. Sometimes, however, it is desirable to also return data from rows that have no matched relationship. For instance, to include products with zero orders in a list of products and ordered quantities.

This can be achieved by adding the OUTER JOIN keywords to a FROM clause, preceded by the LEFT or RIGHT keyword.

When LEFT OUTER JOIN is specified, all the rows in the table specified to the left of this statement are joined to the table on its right. Conversely, when RIGHT OUTER JOIN is specified, all the rows in the table specified to the right of this statement are joined to the table on its left. In each case the conditional test is now stated after the ON keyword, not in a WHERE clause.

This example demonstrates OUTER JOINS, in both directions, to return data from rows that would normally be ignored by a standard inner join.

*outer-join.sql*
*(part of)*

```
# use the "my_database" database
USE my_database;

# create a table called "products" with 3 records
CREATE TABLE IF NOT EXISTS products
( id INT PRIMARY KEY, name CHAR(20) NOT NULL );
INSERT INTO products (id, name) VALUES (111, "Socket");
INSERT INTO products (id, name) VALUES (222, "Widget");
INSERT INTO products (id, name)
  VALUES (333, "Sprocket");

# create a table called "orders" with 3 records
CREATE TABLE IF NOT EXISTS orders
(
  num       INT               PRIMARY KEY,
  product   INT,
  qty       INT,
  client    CHAR(20)
);

INSERT INTO orders (num, product, qty, client)
  VALUES (3570, 222, 1000, "Archie");
```

*The syntax to perform an outer join does vary between DBMS' – refer to the documentation for your own DBMS if it does not support the OUTER JOIN keywords featured in this example.*

*outer-join.sql*
*(cont'd)*

```
INSERT INTO orders (num, client)
  VALUES (5223, "Bernie");
INSERT INTO orders (num, product, qty, client)
  VALUES (4364, 111, 800, "Connie");

# display all products - including those with no orders
SELECT      p.name    AS Product,
            o.num     AS OrderNumber,
            o.qty     AS Quantity,
            o.client  AS Client
FROM        products  AS p LEFT OUTER JOIN orders AS o
ON          p.id = o.product ORDER BY p.name;

# display all orders - including those with no products
SELECT      o.num     AS OrderNumber,
            p.name    AS Product,
            o.qty     AS Quantity,
            o.client  AS Client
FROM        products  AS p RIGHT OUTER JOIN orders AS o
ON          p.id = o.product ORDER BY o.num;

# delete these sample tables
DROP TABLE IF EXISTS products;
DROP TABLE IF EXISTS orders;
```

*When a join is used in a SELECT statement always include a join condition – for any type of join.*

```
MySQL Command Line Client                    _ □ ✕

mysql> source C:\SQL\outer-join.sql
Database changed
+-----------+-------------+----------+---------+
| Product   | OrderNumber | Quantity | Client  |
+-----------+-------------+----------+---------+
| Socket    |        4364 |      800 | Connie  |
| Sprocket  |        NULL |     NULL | NULL    |
| Widget    |        3570 |     1000 | Archie  |
+-----------+-------------+----------+---------+
3 rows in set (0.05 sec)

+-------------+---------+----------+---------+
| OrderNumber | Product | Quantity | Client  |
+-------------+---------+----------+---------+
|        3570 | Widget  |     1000 | Archie  |
|        4364 | Socket  |      800 | Connie  |
|        5223 | NULL    |     NULL | Bernie  |
+-------------+---------+----------+---------+
3 rows in set (0.01 sec)
```

# Summary

- A join creates associations between multiple tables within a single SELECT statement

- One SELECT query can return data from multiple tables by dynamically joining those tables

- It is more efficient to store duplicating data items in a separate table, then define its relationship to another table by identity

- The efficient storage of data in numerous related tables is the essence of good relational database design

- Relational database tables preclude the need to repeatedly input the same data – and they occupy less space too

- Data stored in a relational database table can be updated by changing just a single record

- Storing data as a single record in a relational table assures its consistency

- The name of tables to join are specified as a comma-separated list in a FROM clause within a SELECT statement

- Whenever a join is required, a join condition must be specified to define the relationship between the two tables

- Where multiple tables are joined, multiple join conditions should define their relationships

- A self join enables a SELECT query to make more than one reference to the same table

- Outer joins can return rows that have no matching relationship

- LEFT OUTER JOIN includes all rows in the table specified to the left of the statement and RIGHT OUTER JOIN includes all rows from the table to its right

- The join condition for an inner join is usually specified in a WHERE clause, whereas the join condition for an outer join appears after the ON keyword instead

# Reference section

For handy reference, this appendix contains examples of the most frequently used SQL statements, together with their syntax requirements. It also lists the SQL keywords which must be avoided when naming database columns and tables.

## Covers

**Appendix**

# SQL statements

The following pages list some of the most frequently used SQL statements, together with a brief description of their purpose and explanation of their required syntax. Also, the page number is given where the statement is first introduced in this book.

---

**ALTER TABLE**

Updates an existing table – precedes one or more alteration statements using the ADD, DROP, or CHANGE keywords [see page 44]

ALTER TABLE *table-name*
  ADD COLUMN *column-name data-type modifiers* ,
  ADD PRIMARY KEY ( *column-name* ) ,
  DROP COLUMN *column-name* ,
  CHANGE *old-column-name new-column-name*
       *data-type modifiers* ;

---

**CREATE DATABASE**

Creates a new database – can be qualified with IF NOT EXISTS to check if a database of the specified name already exists [see page 24]

CREATE DATABASE IF NOT EXISTS *database-name* ;

---

**CREATE TABLE**

Creates a new database table – precedes parentheses specifying name, data type and optional modifiers for each column. It can be qualified with IF NOT EXISTS to check if a table of the specified name already exists [see page 34]

CREATE TABLE IF NOT EXISTS *table-name*
  ( *column-name data-type modifiers* ,
    *column-name data-type modifiers* ) ;

**DELETE FROM**
Permanently deletes one or more rows from a table – requires a WHERE clause to identify the row/s to delete. It will delete all rows without warning if a WHERE clause is omitted [see page 58]

DELETE FROM *table-name* ;
DELETE FROM *table-name* WHERE *column = value* ;

**DROP DATABASE**
Permanently deletes an existing database – can be qualified with IF EXISTS to check that a database of the specified name does indeed exist [see page 26]

DROP DATABASE IF EXISTS *database-name* ;

**DROP TABLE**
Permanently deletes an existing database table – can be qualified with IF EXISTS to check that a table of the specified name does indeed exist [see page 36]

DROP TABLE *table-name* ;
DROP TABLE IF EXISTS *table-name* ;

**EXPLAIN**
Reveals the format of the specified table, listing column names, data types and optional modifiers [see page 33]

EXPLAIN *table-name* ;

**GRANT**

Grant statements can create a new user and assign various levels of access privileges. A user's level of privileges can be examined with a SHOW GRANTS statement [see page 130]

GRANT ALL PRIVILEGES ON *.* TO *user@domain* IDENTIFIED BY " *password* " WITH GRANT OPTION ;

SHOW GRANTS FOR *user@domain* ;

**INSERT INTO**

Inserts a record into an existing table – precedes the VALUES keyword followed by parentheses containing a comma-separated list of data values. These must match the number of columns and be of appropriate data types [see page 48]

INSERT INTO *table-name* VALUES ( *value* , *value* , *value* ) ;

A recommended option allows a column list to specify where data should be inserted [see page 50]

INSERT INTO *table-name* ( *column* , *column* , *column* )
  VALUES ( *value* , *value* , *value* ) ;

Data can be copied from one table into another by replacing the VALUES list with a SELECT statement – the data types must be appropriate in each column [see page 52]

INSERT INTO   *destination-table-name*
        ( *column* , *column* , *column* )
        SELECT * FROM *source-table-name* ;

## SELECT FROM

Retrieves specified data from an existing database table. The *
wildcard character returns the entire data stored there or data
can be returned for one or more columns by stating their names
as a comma-separated list [see page 62]

SELECT * FROM *table-name* ;
SELECT *column-name* FROM *table-name* ;
SELECT *column* , *column* , *column* FROM *table-name* ;


A WHERE clause can be added to a SELECT statement to
identify a particular row or rows [see page 66]

SELECT * FROM *table-name* WHERE *column* = *value* ;


An ORDER BY clause can be added to the end of a SELECT
statement to determine the alphabetic or numeric order in which
the data returned by the query is sorted [see page 74]

SELECT * FROM *table-name* ORDER BY *column-name* ;


Data sort order can be explicitly set as ascending or descending
by adding the ASC or DESC keyword at the end of an
ORDER BY clause – if not specified, ascending order is assumed
[see page 80]

SELECT * FROM *table-name*
  ORDER BY *column-name* DESC ;


A WHERE clause can compare data in multiple columns with the
OR and AND logical operators [see page 96]

SELECT * FROM *table-name*
  WHERE *column-name* = *value*
  AND *column-name* = *value* ;

**SELECT FROM** (continued)

Column data can be compared against multiple inclusive alternatives with the IN keyword – this precedes parentheses containing the comma-separated list of alternative values. Similarly, multiple exclusive values can be compared with the NOT IN keywords [see page 100]

SELECT * FROM *table-name*
  WHERE *column-name* IN ( *value* , *value* , *value* )
  AND *column-name* NOT IN ( *value* , *value* , *value* ) ;

Textual column data can be compared against a search pattern using the LIKE keyword – the query will return all matches that are similar to the specified pattern [see page 104]

SELECT * FROM *table-name*
  WHERE *column-name* LIKE *search-pattern* ;

Alias names can be specified for columns with the AS keyword [see page 116]

SELECT *column-name-1* AS *col1* ,
        *column-name-2* AS *col2*
        FROM *table-name* ;

Data returned by a SELECT query can be grouped around the column specified in a GROUP BY clause [see page 142]

SELECT * FROM *table-name*
GROUP BY *column-name* ;

Grouped data can be filtered with a HAVING clause – row data is filtered by the WHERE clause [see page 144]

SELECT * FROM *table-name*
GROUP BY *column-name*
HAVING *expression* ;

### SHOW DATABASES
Lists the names of all databases in the DBMS [see page 23]

SHOW DATABASES ;

### SHOW TABLES
Lists the name of all tables within the currently selected database [see page 32]

SHOW TABLES ;

### UPDATE
Replaces data in one or more columns of a table – precedes a SET statement specifying one or more columns and values. It requires a WHERE clause to identify the row/s to update otherwise it will update all rows without warning [see page 56]

UPDATE *table-name* SET *column-name = value* ;
UPDATE *table-name*
  SET *column-name = value* , *column-name = value*
  WHERE *column = value* ;

### USE
Selects a database in which to add, manipulate or retrieve table data [see page 32]

USE *database-name* ;

# SQL reserved words

The following tables in the remainder of this appendix list keywords that have special meaning in SQL. These are known as "reserved" words and should not be used when naming databases, tables, columns or any other objects within a SQL database – using a keyword in a name will generate an error.

DBMS' tend to support a specific set of keywords so not all the keywords listed in these tables are supported by any one DBMS – each DBMS will support a subset of this list.

In addition to the keywords listed in the following tables, some DBMS' have further extended this list of SQL reserved words with their own implementation-specific keywords. The documentation for each DBMS will normally list all the keywords that it supports.

Except for their intended purpose, it is strongly recommended that the use of all reserved words should be avoided – even those which are not currently supported by your own DBMS. This should ensure that the SQL code remains portable and compatible with new releases of all DBMS'.

| | | |
|---|---|---|
| ABSOLUTE | ASC | BIT |
| ACTION | ASCENDING | BLOB |
| ACTIVE | ASSERTION | BOOLEAN |
| ADD | AT | BOTH |
| AFTER | AUTHORIZATION | BREAK |
| ALL | AUTO | BROWSE |
| ALLOCATE | AUTOINC | BULK |
| ALTER | AVG | BY |
| AND | BACKUP | BYTES |
| ANY | BEFORE | CACHE |
| ARE | BEGIN | CASCADE |
| AS | BETWEEN | CASCADED |

| | | |
|---|---|---|
| CASE | CONTINUE | DISCONNECT |
| CAST | CONTROLROW | DISK |
| CATALOG | CONVERT | DISTINCT |
| CHAR | COUNT | DISTRIBUTED |
| CHARACTER | CREATE | DO |
| CHECK | CROSS | DOMAIN |
| CHECKPOINT | CSTRING | DOUBLE |
| CLOSE | CUBE | DROP |
| CLUSTERED | CURRENT | DUMMY |
| COALESCE | CURSOR | DUMP |
| COLLATE | DATABASE | ELSE |
| COLUMN | DATE | END |
| COMMENT | DATETIME | ERRLVL |
| COMMIT | DAY | ERROREXIT |
| COMMITTED | DBCC | ESCAPE |
| COMPUTE | DEALLOCATE | EXCEPT |
| COMPUTED | DEBUG | EXCEPTION |
| CONDITIONAL | DEC | EXEC |
| CONFIRM | DECIMAL | EXECUTE |
| CONNECT | DECLARE | EXISTS |
| CONNECTION | DEFAULT | EXIT |
| CONSTRAINT | DELETE | EXTERNAL |
| CONSTRAINTS | DENY | EXTRACT |
| CONTAINING | DESC | FALSE |
| CONTAINS | DESCENDING | FETCH |
| CONTAINSTABLE | DESCRIBE | FILE |

| FILLFACTOR | INDICATOR | LOWER |
| --- | --- | --- |
| FILTER | INNER | MANUAL |
| FLOAT | INPUT | MATCH |
| FLOPPY | INSERT | MAX |
| FOR | INT | MERGE |
| FOREIGN | INTEGER | MESSAGE |
| FOUND | INTERSECT | MIN |
| FREETEXT | INTERVAL | MINUTE |
| FREETEXTTABLE | INTO | MIRROREXIT |
| FROM | IS | MODULE |
| FULL | ISOLATION | MONEY |
| FUNCTION | JOIN | MONTH |
| GENERATOR | KEY | NAMES |
| GET | KILL | NATIONAL |
| GO | LANGUAGE | NATURAL |
| GOTO | LAST | NCHAR |
| GRANT | LEADING | NEXT |
| GROUP | LEFT | NO |
| HAVING | LENGTH | NOCHECK |
| HOLDLOCK | LEVEL | NONCLUSTERED |
| HOUR | LIKE | NONE |
| IDENTITY | LINENO | NOT |
| IF | LOAD | NULL |
| IN | LOCAL | NULLIF |
| INACTIVE | LOGFILE | NUMERIC |
| INDEX | LONG | OF |

| OFF | PREPARE | ROLLBACK |
|-----|---------|----------|
| OFFSETS | PRIMARY | ROLLUP |
| ON | PRINT | ROWCOUNT |
| ONCE | PRIOR | RULE |
| ONLY | PRIVILEGES | SAVE |
| OPEN | PROC | SCHEMA |
| OPTION | PROCEDURE | SECOND |
| OR | PROCESSEXIT | SECTION |
| ORDER | PROTECTED | SEGMENT |
| OUTER | PUBLIC | SELECT |
| OUTPUT | RAISERROR | SEQUENCE |
| OVER | READ | SET |
| OVERFLOW | READTEXT | SETUSER |
| PAD | REAL | SHADOW |
| PAGE | REFERENCES | SHARED |
| PAGES | RELATIVE | SHUTDOWN |
| PARAMETER | REPLICATION | SINGULAR |
| PARTIAL | RESERV | SIZE |
| PASSWORD | RESERVING | SMALLINT |
| PERCENT | RESTORE | SNAPSHOT |
| PERM | RESTRICT | SOME |
| PERMANENT | RETAIN | SORT |
| PIPE | RETURN | SPACE |
| PLAN | RETURNS | SQL |
| POSITION | REVOKE | SQLCODE |
| PRECISION | RIGHT | SQLERROR |

| | | |
|---|---|---|
| STABILITY | TRAILING | VALUE |
| STARTING | TRAN | VALUES |
| STARTS | TRANSACTION | VARCHAR |
| STATISTICS | TRANSLATE | VARIABLE |
| SUBSTRING | TRIGGER | VARYING |
| SUM | TRIM | VIEW |
| SUSPEND | TRUE | VOLUME |
| TABLE | TRUNCATE | WAIT |
| TAPE | UNCOMMITTED | WAITFOR |
| TEMP | UNION | WHEN |
| TEMPORARY | UNIQUE | WHERE |
| TEXT | UPDATE | WHILE |
| TEXTSIZE | UPDATETEXT | WITH |
| THEN | UPPER | WORK |
| TIME | USAGE | WRITE |
| TIMESTAMP | USE | WRITETEXT |
| TO | USER | YEAR |
| TOP | USING | ZONE |

# Index

# D

# E

# F

# G

# H

# I

# J

# K